Massachusetts
Legal Research

CAROLINA ACADEMIC PRESS
LEGAL RESEARCH SERIES

Suzanne E. Rowe, Series Editor

❧

Arizona, Second Edition—Tamara S. Herrera

Arkansas, Second Edition—Coleen M. Barger, Cheryl L. Reinhart &
Cathy L. Underwood

California, Third Edition—Aimee Dudovitz, Hether C. Macfarlane
& Suzanne E. Rowe

Colorado—Robert Michael Linz

Connecticut—Jessica G. Hynes

Federal, Second Edition—Mary Garvey Algero, Spencer L. Simons,
Suzanne E. Rowe, Scott Childs & Sarah E. Ricks

Florida, Fourth Edition—Barbara J. Busharis, Jennifer LaVia & Suzanne E. Rowe

Georgia—Nancy P. Johnson, Elizabeth G. Adelman & Nancy J. Adams

Idaho, Second Edition—Tenielle Fordyce-Ruff & Kristina J. Running

Illinois, Second Edition—Mark E. Wojcik

Iowa, Second Edition—John D. Edwards, Karen L. Wallace & Melissa H. Weresh

Kansas—Joseph A. Custer & Christopher L. Steadham

Kentucky—William A. Hilyerd, Kurt X. Metzmeier & David J. Ensign

Louisiana, Second Edition—Mary Garvey Algero

Massachusetts, Second Edition—E. Joan Blum & Shaun B. Spencer

Michigan, Third Edition—Pamela Lysaght & Cristina D. Lockwood

Minnesota—Suzanne Thorpe

Mississippi—Kristy L. Gilliland

Missouri, Third Edition—Wanda M. Temm & Julie M. Cheslik

New York, Third Edition—Elizabeth G. Adelman, Theodora Belniak
Courtney L. Selby & Brian Detweiler

North Carolina, Second Edition—Scott Childs & Sara Sampson

North Dakota—Anne Mullins & Tammy Pettinato

Ohio, Second Edition—Sara Sampson, Katherine L. Hall
& Carolyn Broering-Jacobs

Oklahoma—Darin K. Fox, Darla W. Jackson & Courtney L. Selby

Oregon, Third Edition Revised Printing—Suzanne E. Rowe

Pennsylvania—Barbara J. Busharis & Bonny L. Tavares

Tennessee, Second Edition—Scott Childs, Sibyl Marshall & Carol McCrehan Parker

Texas, Second Edition—Spencer L. Simons

Washington, Second Edition—Julie Heintz-Cho, Tom Cobb
& Mary A. Hotchkiss

West Virginia—Hollee Schwartz Temple

Wisconsin—Patricia Cervenka & Leslie Behroozi

Wyoming, Second Edition—Debora A. Person & Tawnya K. Plumb

❧

Massachusetts Legal Research

Second Edition

E. Joan Blum
Shaun B. Spencer

Suzanne E. Rowe, Series Editor

Carolina Academic Press
Durham, North Carolina

Library of Congress Cataloging-in-Publication Data

Names: Blum, E. Joan, author. | Spencer, Shaun B., author.
Title: Massachusetts legal research / E. Joan Blum, Shaun B. Spencer.
Description: Second Edition. | Durham, North Carolina : Carolina Academic
    Press, [2016] | Series: Legal research series | Includes bibliographical
    references and index.
Identifiers: LCCN 2016027854 | ISBN 9781611637618 (alk. paper)
Subjects: LCSH: Legal research--Massachusetts.
Classification: LCC KFM2475 .B58 2016 | DDC 340.072/0744--dc23
LC record available at https://lccn.loc.gov/2016027854

Carolina Academic Press, LLC
700 Kent Street
Durham, North Carolina 27701
Telephone (919) 489-7486
Fax (919) 493-5668
www.cap-press.com

Printed in the United States of America

To Dan
E.J.B.

To Deb, for believing in me
S.B.S.

Summary of Contents

Contents

List of Tables and Figures

Tables

Figures

Series Note

The Legal Research Series published by Carolina Academic Press includes titles from states around the country as well as a separate text on federal legal research. The goal of each book is to provide law students, practitioners, para-legals, college students, laypeople, and librarians with the essential elements of legal research in each jurisdiction. Unlike more bibliographic texts, the Legal Research Series books seek to explain concisely both the sources of legal research and the process for conducting legal research effectively.

Preface and Acknowledgments

Legal research is a complex skill. Competent legal research requires ongoing analysis as well as mastery of a knowledge base and of techniques for using it. While some tools of legal research change — sometimes with breathtaking speed — the basics of legal research remain the same. An effective research process continues to include analyzing a problem carefully to identify issues to research, choosing research tools and using them efficiently to identify relevant legal authorities, and then analyzing and applying those authorities to the problem.

Legal researchers have always benefited from advances in technology. These advances affect the way legal authorities are distributed and how we find them. Given the constant evolution of online legal research services, we have minimized the degree to which we address the specifics of existing services. Instead, we emphasize general functions and strategies to help you conduct effective legal research regardless of which service you use.

For this book, we were privileged to work closely with Suzanne Rowe, the editor of the Legal Research Series. Suzanne is a masterful and compassionate editor whose contributions to our work have been invaluable. Some of the general explanations in our book are drawn from earlier editions of *Oregon Legal Research*, authored by Suzanne, and are used with permission. We are indebted to Joan Shear of the Boston College Law Library and to Spencer Clough of the University of Massachusetts School of Law Library for their assistance with this book and their collaboration over many years of teaching legal research.

Our thinking about legal research as a process and its relationship with legal analysis and writing has developed over our combined four decades of teaching legal research and writing at Boston College Law School, Harvard Law School, and the University of Massachusetts School of Law. We are grateful for the support of the Boston College Law School Fund and the University of Massachusetts School of Law Summer Research Program, both of which made it possible for us to complete this book.

Massachusetts
Legal Research

Chapter 1

Introduction to Legal Research

I. Legal Research: A Core Component of Legal Problem Solving

A. Legal Problem Solving and the Work of the Lawyer

Lawyers' work includes a very wide range of professional activities. These activities include advising clients, arguing on behalf of clients before a court, negotiating transactions, ensuring compliance with regulations, drafting legislation, lobbying lawmakers, and advocating for the disadvantaged. Lawyers' professional activities require numerous lawyering skills, but all these professional activities rest on the foundation of legal problem solving.

In the most general terms, a lawyer engages in legal problem solving by identifying the law that is relevant to a particular problem and applying that law in the given context. In the advisory context, the lawyer engages in problem solving when she identifies the relevant law and assesses how a court would likely apply it to her client's situation. In the advocacy context, problem solving involves, in addition to those steps, identifying and evaluating potential arguments. In the transactional context, the lawyer who negotiates a deal and drafts documents solves problems when he drafts in light of the legal and factual context of the transaction. In the compliance context, the lawyer solves problems when she decides how to apply a regulatory framework to a specific set of facts. Analyzing and applying existing law to a given situation is also part of the work of the lawyer who drafts legislation, lobbies on behalf of a client, or represents the disadvantaged.

B. Legal Research and Legal Problem Solving

Legal research is an essential component of legal problem solving because it is through the process of legal research that the lawyer identifies the law that applies in a particular situation. To fully address a legal problem, the lawyer must also analyze and apply the applicable law.

While legal research is the foundation of legal problem solving, the relationship between these operations is not necessarily linear. Yes, the lawyer must identify the applicable law before coming up with a solution to a legal problem. But how does the lawyer know what law applies in a given situation? Figuring this out is a process that itself requires decision-making at every step, although novice legal researchers may need to approach this task more deliberately than experts do. Legal research is an iterative process through which the lawyer explores possibilities, analyzes those possibilities to make tentative findings, and explores further possibilities in light of those findings.

To begin the research process, you must identify the legal issues raised by the problem by analyzing the facts in light of what you already know. This knowledge may come from experience in law school or law practice or even from non-legal sources. Then, using your knowledge in connection with the specific information base and techniques of legal research, you must first cast a wide net to identify legal authority that is *potentially* relevant. Analyzing that material helps you refine your understanding of the legal problem, which in turn helps you discriminate among potentially relevant authorities to eventually identify those that are most relevant to your problem. This process of building on what you learn continues until you are satisfied that you have uncovered all the law that applies to the problem and that it is appropriate to move on to the next stage of the problem-solving process. Thus, as with many other lawyering skills, the skill of legal research requires mastery of specific information and techniques as well as application of general analytical skills.

II. About This Book

A. The Focus of This Book: Massachusetts Law

The fundamentals of legal research are the same in every American jurisdiction, although the details vary. Most variations in research process are minor. A lawyer who is familiar with Massachusetts legal research will ordinarily not find it difficult to adjust to researching federal law or the law of another state. In some instances, however, researching the law of a specific jurisdiction requires specialized knowledge of the resources available and of the analytical framework in which those resources are used.[1] This book focuses on how to

---

1. For example, unlike the federal law of evidence and the law of most states, the Massachusetts law of evidence is uncodified. *See* Mark S. Brodin & Michael Avery,

do effective and efficient legal research into Massachusetts law. The book includes some examples of research in federal sources to introduce those sources as well as to highlight variations. It also includes some examples from the law of other states. It does not, however, go into non-Massachusetts materials in detail.

B. The Organization of This Book

This chapter introduces you to legal research at the most general level by addressing the importance of legal research in the professional life of the lawyer and providing an introduction to legal authority. Chapter 2 introduces you to the process of legal research. The remainder of this book introduces you specifically to Massachusetts legal research resources and the techniques for using them in print and in online media. Although research into federal law or the law of other states involves different sources and may involve different techniques, you will be able to extrapolate from what you learn here about Massachusetts legal research to research problems arising under the law of most other U.S. jurisdictions.

Chapter 3 introduces secondary sources, some specific to Massachusetts and some that are more general, and discusses the place of secondary sources in legal research. Chapters 4 and 5 address judicial opinions, including the role of "citators," tools that help researchers assess the validity and track the history of cases and other legal authorities. Chapter 6 addresses statutes, and Chapter 7 examines the legislative process and legislative history research. Chapter 8 addresses Massachusetts administrative law research, Chapter 9 discusses the Massachusetts Constitution, and Chapter 10 discusses rules of evidence, procedure, and professional conduct. Appendix A provides an overview of the conventions lawyers use in citing authority, and Appendix B discusses techniques for constructing full-text searches in online legal research services. Appendix C is a selected bibliography of books on general legal research.

Handbook of Massachusetts Evidence 2016 Edition § 1.1 (Wolters Kluwer 2015). Thus, researching the Massachusetts law of evidence requires an approach that is different from researching the federal law of evidence or the law of most other states.

III. Legal Authority: The Foundation of Legal Research

A working definition of "law" is an official statement of a government unit. In legal parlance, the term "authority" generally refers to the law that explains, supports, or requires a particular position, but sometimes "authority" refers to secondary sources, materials that are not law. The classifications of authority—as primary or secondary, and mandatory or persuasive—inform the lawyer about the status and weight of a particular authority in a given situation.

A. Types of Authority

Primary authority is *law*. Sources of primary authority are documents such as constitutions, statutes, cases, regulations, and executive orders. Secondary authority is material written *about the law* by scholars, practitioners, and others to help us understand the law or argue for changes in the law. Secondary authority can be found in a variety of sources including books, journal and law review articles, specialized legal materials, speeches, explanatory materials, and so forth.

Different government units make law in different forms. The Massachusetts Constitution is amended by a joint session of the Commonwealth's[2] legislature sitting in constitutional convention. The state legislature[3] enacts statutes. The courts of the Commonwealth decide cases to resolve legal disputes; decisions in appellate cases are sources of law for future cases. Courts also issue rules of court. Upon request, the Supreme Judicial Court, the highest court of the Commonwealth, may issue advisory opinions to the Governor or to the legislature.

Although today many areas of law are governed by statute, some areas remain controlled entirely by case law, which is sometimes referred to as "judge-made" or "common" law. Municipalities within the Commonwealth enact ordinances or adopt by-laws. State agencies promulgate regulations, and the Governor issues executive orders.

---

2. Massachusetts is one of four states in the United States to use the official title of "Commonwealth" rather than "State." (The other three are Pennsylvania, Kentucky, and Virginia.) It is so designated in the Massachusetts Constitution, which is entitled "A Constitution or Form of Government for the Commonwealth of Massachusetts." Although the title "Commonwealth" may indicate a special commitment to the public good, the title has little, if any, practical significance, as Massachusetts has the same position and powers within the United States as other states.

3. For historical reasons, the Massachusetts legislature is formally called the "General Court."

B. Weight of Authority and the Importance of Precedent

Mandatory (or "binding") authority is the law that a court must follow. Even though only a small percentage of legal matters are litigated, the lawyer must solve problems on the basis of an assessment of what a court *would* decide if the matter were to be litigated. This assessment includes how the court would apply a statute or regulation as well as how the court would apply judge-made law. Thus, to varying degrees, the court is always in the background of a lawyer's problem solving, even when a problem is governed by statutes and regulations.

One reason why legal research is so important is that courts take precedent into account in almost every case. Our system of adjudication rests on the principle of *stare decisis*, a Latin term meaning "to stand by things decided."[4] Therefore, a court is guided by what has been decided in previous cases, or "precedent," in order to resolve the case before it. The notion of precedent, which promotes consistency in judicial decision-making and therefore predictability in matters touched by law, is an extremely important concept in the U.S. legal system.

In areas not governed by statute, precedent derived from cases determines the law that applies to the case. Courts also look to precedent when there is an applicable statute. When a statute applies to the case before a court, the court decides the case by applying and, if necessary, interpreting the statute. In theory, statutes are a series of explicit commands that mean what they say and say what they mean. In practice, however, statutory language may be vague or ambiguous or riddled with inconsistencies or gaps. When a court interprets a statute, the court looks first to the text of the statute and may look to other interpretive aids.[5] When past cases have grappled with the same or similar interpretive questions, the court relies on these precedent cases to interpret the statute.

Only primary authority may be binding, and only within its jurisdiction. Federal law is binding throughout the United States. Massachusetts primary

---

4. *Black's Law Dictionary* 1626 (10th ed. 2014).

5. Judges and scholars hold differing views on the problem of statutory interpretation. These views range from textualism to purposivism, with fine gradations in between. References to scholarly writings on this topic can be found throughout Peter L. Strauss, *Legislation — Understanding and Using Statutes* (Found. Press 2005). For a case with a majority opinion and a dissent reflecting different approaches to statutory interpretation, see *King v. Burwell*, 135 S. Ct. 2480 (2015). For a case with a majority opinion and two dissents reflecting a range of judicial approaches to interpreting the Constitution, see *District of Columbia v. Heller*, 554 U.S. 570 (2008).

authority—a Massachusetts statute or case, for example—is ordinarily binding only within Massachusetts.[6] Table 1-1 gives an example of a federal statute, which is binding throughout the United States, and a Massachusetts statute, which is binding only within Massachusetts.

Table 1-1. Binding Authority

Federal law — binding across the U.S.	State law — binding only within the state
The United States Congress enacted the Individuals with Disabilities Education Act (IDEA), which entitles special education students in all fifty states to a free and appropriate education. This act is binding authority in every state.	The Massachusetts legislature enacted legislation to require all public school students to earn a passing score on the Massachusetts Comprehensive Assessment System (MCAS) test in order to earn a high school diploma. The MCAS statute is binding only in the Commonwealth of Massachusetts.

Persuasive authority is authority that is not binding, but that nonetheless may be used to explain or to persuade. Persuasive authority may include primary authority from other jurisdictions as well as secondary authority. In *Lewis v. Lewis*, 370 Mass. 619 (1976), the Supreme Judicial Court of Massachusetts abrogated the doctrine of inter-spousal tort immunity, which, until then, had prevented one spouse from suing the other in tort. In reaching its decision to change this legal rule, the court relied on two types of persuasive authority: cases from other jurisdictions (primary persuasive authority) and scholarly writings (secondary authority).

Within a jurisdiction, primary authorities have a hierarchical relationship. This means that when different types of mandatory authority bear on a legal problem, some have priority over others. The constitution of a state is the supreme law of that state and thus must be considered first. If a statute of the

---

6. But a court may apply the law of a state other than the state in which the court sits when the other state has a greater connection with the matter at issue. "Problems arise when legally significant aspects of a case are divided between two or more states.... Suppose that A injures B in state Y and B brings suit against A in state X to recover for his injuries. If the local law rules of X and Y differ in relevant respects, the X court may be called upon to decide whether to apply the rules of one state rather than the rules of the other." *Restatement (Second) Conflict of Laws* § 1 cmt. b (1971). The body of law that governs how a decision is made in this situation is referred to as the law of conflicts of law. For more about restatements of the law see Chapter 3, which discusses secondary sources.

state is on point, the statute comes next in the hierarchy, followed by administrative regulations. Judicial opinions come next: A judicial opinion may apply or interpret the statute or regulation but cannot disregard it. A judicial opinion may, however, hold that a statute is unconstitutional or that an administrative regulation is beyond the authority of the issuing agency. If no constitutional provision, statute, or administrative regulation is on point, then the issue is governed by case law. Table 1-2 shows some of the types of authority a Massachusetts legal researcher encounters and the hierarchy of Massachusetts primary authority.

Table 1-2. Examples of Authority in Massachusetts Research

	Mandatory Authority	Persuasive Authority
Primary Authority	• (Applicable federal materials) • Massachusetts Constitution • Massachusetts statutes and regulations • Massachusetts Supreme Judicial Court cases	• Rhode Island Supreme Court decisions • Decisions of federal courts on purely state-law issues
Secondary Authority	(Secondary authority is never mandatory.)	• Practice guides • Law review articles • Legal encyclopedias

The place of a court in the judicial hierarchy determines the weight of authority of its decisions. In brief: A lower court is bound by the decisions of courts above it in the jurisdiction's court hierarchy. The courts of most jurisdictions within the United States follow a similar model, with trial courts at the lowest level, intermediate appellate courts in the middle, and a court of last resort at the top. Figure 1-1 sets out a simplified diagram of Massachusetts court structure.[7] There are no courts below the trial courts in the court hierarchy, so decisions of Massachusetts trial courts are not binding, although, like many other materials, they may sometimes be persuasive.

---

7. For a chart offering a detailed description of the Massachusetts court system, go to www.mass.gov/courts/docs/sjc/docs/court-sys-chart-2012.pdf.

Figure 1-1. Simplified Diagram of Massachusetts Court Hierarchy

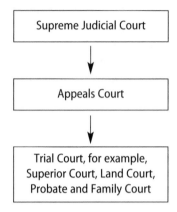

Arrows indicate that decisions are binding on courts below.

Chapter 2

Legal Research as a Process

I. Introduction

A lawyer who sets out to find the authorities that govern a given problem encounters a wealth of materials. Multiple gateways — law libraries, free internet resources, commercial research services — provide access to many other resources, including finding tools and primary and secondary authorities, some of which are available both in print and online. Faced with these choices, the lawyer's first question is where to start; the second question is how to proceed.

Legal research is a process of investigation that requires you to reflect on and learn from the steps you take. There are tasks that you should perform, or consider performing, in every research project, but you may not always perform those tasks in the same order.

This chapter gives an overview of a general research process that you can adapt to different problems and to your own learning style. That process breaks down into three broad phases: an initial phase, in which you orient yourself to your project and make preliminary decisions about research strategy; a second phase, in which you identify and evaluate potentially relevant authority; and a third phase, in which you check your research to make sure it is comprehensive and up-to-date.

This chapter is designed to be read several times. First, read it all the way through to get an overview of the process of legal research and gain insight into how interconnected are the available operations and resources. Then, as you read through the later chapters of this book and learn about specific resources and techniques, return to this chapter to remind yourself how you can use those resources and operations in an effective and efficient research process.

II. First Phase: Getting Oriented

Before starting to look for the authority that governs your problem, take the time to orient yourself to your problem by thinking carefully, in a general way, about the legal issues and about the controlling jurisdiction. Taking this preliminary step will increase the efficiency of your research by giving you an overview of your project. This, in turn, will help you identify fruitful research paths and avoid unproductive ones.

A. Step #1: Identify the Legal Issues

For your research strategy to be effective, you must first identify, at least as a preliminary matter, the legal issues to research. A supervisor may explicitly identify the issues for you. When you work without a supervisor or your supervisor does not tell you what issues to research, you must identify the issues yourself based on the context of your representation of the client, your understanding of the facts, and your prior experience.

Always be open to redefining the issues as you proceed with your research, even when your supervisor defines the project for you. As you research, you will gradually gain expertise in the specific area you are researching. Even if your supervisor is an expert in the general area, your research may give you the opportunity to reflect in greater depth than your supervisor about the potential application of the law to the specific facts of the problem you are researching. Your growing expertise may require you to modify the way you initially identified the issues. Thus, even when your supervisor identifies issues, be on the lookout for other possibilities and do not hesitate to bring fresh insights to the attention of your supervisor. This is essential to effective representation of your client.

Most research projects begin with a set of facts.[1] Facts come from various sources, including memos, documents, interviews with clients, or conversations with your supervisor. Even when you suspect that the initial facts you receive do not provide a complete picture of the client's problem, you must nonetheless begin your research with the facts you have. Through your research, you will refine your understanding of the relevant law and seek additional or more specific facts.

For example, you may use information from a client interview to identify legal issues and assess the likelihood that your client has a cause of action. Your

---

1. But not all projects begin this way—sometimes a lawyer is asked by a supervisor to assemble all the legislation on a particular topic or to find all the cases citing a particular case (or to perform some other similar function).

client, Max Roberts, tells you that he wants to sue a restaurant because he found a chicken bone at the bottom of a bowl of soup he ate there. Mr. Roberts consumes no animal products on advice of his health practitioner. He ate at the restaurant specifically because in its advertising and menus the restaurant represented itself as a vegan establishment, serving no products of animal origin. Mr. Roberts did not suffer any immediate physical harm, but he is upset and angry that the restaurant served him food that was not vegan.

Organized brainstorming is an effective way to identify legal issues raised by a set of facts. One tried and true method of organized brainstorming is asking yourself a standard set of questions about the facts. Some researchers ask journalistic questions: Who? What? Why? When? Where? How? Others use a specifically legal mnemonic device called TARPP, which stands for Things, Actions, Remedies, People, and Places.[2] Table 2-1 shows how to use these two approaches to help you identify the legal issues raised by your client's problem.

Table 2-1. Identify Issues by Asking Specific Questions

Journalistic Approach	
Who:	Restaurant patron, business, consumer, vegan
What:	Food, menu, advertisement
How:	Misleading, false, deceptive
Why:	Consumer protection, false advertising
When:	Current
Where:	Restaurant, business, Massachusetts
TARPP Approach	
Things:	Food, menu, advertisement
Actions:	Consumer protection, false advertising
Remedies:	Injunction, damages
People:	Restaurant patron, business, consumer, vegan
Places:	Restaurant, business, Massachusetts

---

2. *See* Steven M. Barkan, Roy M. Mersky & Donald J. Dunn, *Fundamentals of Legal Research* 20 (10th ed., Found. Press 2015) (explaining TARPP, a similar mnemonic device).

Some researchers may find it more helpful simply to reflect generally on the facts and their own experience to arrive at a preliminary identification of the issues. Table 2-2 illustrates how you might reflect generally to come to a preliminary identification of issues to research.

Table 2-2. Identify Issues by Reflecting Generally

Based on the facts you learn from the interview with Mr. Roberts, you make a preliminary decision that he does not have a viable cause of action in tort or in contract. The fact that he relied on the restaurant's advertising leads you to consider the possibility that he has a remedy under specific laws relating to false advertising or more general consumer protection laws. As a preliminary matter, you decide to pursue these lines of research.

B. Step #2: Identify the Controlling Jurisdiction(s)

Identifying the controlling jurisdiction is a crucial step in the orientation phase of a research project. Is the issue controlled by federal law or by state law? If it is a state law issue, is it governed by the law of Massachusetts or by the law of another state? This step is very important because, to research effectively, you must narrow your research to the law of the appropriate jurisdiction(s).

The U.S. Constitution empowers the federal government to make law only in certain areas.[3] While the scope of federal lawmaking expanded dramatically in the twentieth century, state law governs a wide range of activities. Thus, you need to decide (again, as a preliminary matter subject to revision as you research) whether federal law or state law, or maybe both,[4] controls your problem. As you gain experience, you will develop an intuitive sense about jurisdiction, but always think carefully about the possibilities.[5]

---

3. These areas include, but are not limited to, coining money, regulating interstate and foreign commerce, and engaging in foreign relations.

4. For example, a real estate developer may have to comply with both federal and state environmental regulations.

5. In *Riegel v. Medtronic Inc.*, 552 U.S. 312 (2008), the plaintiff's lawyer may not initially have considered the possibility that federal law would be relevant when the plaintiff, who was seriously injured when a medical device failed, sued under New York tort law in New York state court. The defendant, the manufacturer, considered the possibility that federal law might apply and eventually argued successfully in the United States Supreme Court that a federal statute, the 1976 Medical Device Amendments Act, preempted state law and thus that the plaintiff had no cause of action under state law.

If you conclude that the matter is not governed by federal law, you will need to answer a further question: which state's law governs? In many situations, it is obvious which state has the greatest interest in a matter, and the law of that state will control.[6] For example, when a person breaks into a house in Holliston, Massachusetts, the law of Massachusetts controls because the Commonwealth of Massachusetts has the greatest interest of any state in crimes committed within its borders. Similarly, when the owner sells that house, ordinarily Massachusetts law controls because Massachusetts has the greatest interest in how property within the state is conveyed. But there may be situations in which another state has a greater interest. For example, the Supreme Judicial Court of Massachusetts held that Texas had a more significant relationship than Massachusetts to a case in which a Massachusetts resident sued an Illinois corporation in Massachusetts state court for injuries sustained at a hotel operated by the corporation in Texas, and thus the trial court in Massachusetts appropriately applied the two-year Texas statute of limitations instead of the three-year Massachusetts statute.[7]

C. Step #3: Test Your Preliminary Assessments

The final step in the orientation phase is to seek "expert help" to test your identification of the issues and the controlling jurisdiction. Expert help most frequently comes in written form from a secondary source, for example, a treatise, practice guide, or law review article. But it might also come from a person: a law librarian, a supervisor, or a colleague.

In whatever form you seek expert help, drawing on expertise at this early stage of your research will contribute to the efficiency and overall effectiveness of your research process. Once you tentatively identify the issues, a secondary source will provide background about the area of law and help confirm that you are on the right track or suggest issues that you did not see earlier.[8] Similarly, a human expert — for example, a law librarian or supervisor — may provide "reality testing" that confirms or challenges the way you have conceptualized the problem. While it is appropriate in almost every situation to seek expert help from a secondary source, it is your responsibility, in a given situ-

---

6. In resolving conflicts of laws, Massachusetts follows the "functional approach" of the *Restatement (Second) of Conflicts of Laws* and applies the local law of the state that has the most significant relationship to the transaction and the parties. *Bushkin Assocs., Inc. v. Raytheon Co.*, 393 Mass. 622, 630–32 (1985).

7. *Nierman v. Hyatt Corp.*, 441 Mass. 693, 698 (2004).

8. Chapter 3 addresses how to find and use secondary sources.

ation, to gauge the appropriateness of seeking help from a human expert. Table 2-3 lists some sources of "expert help" you might turn to in the preliminary phase of a research project.

Table 2-3. Some Sources of "Expert Help"

"Expert help" can come from a written secondary source, for example:	"Expert help" can come from a person, for example:
A practice guide A treatise A law review article	A law librarian A supervisor A colleague

III. Second Phase: Finding and Evaluating Potentially Binding Authority

The goal of your research process is to assemble the body of authority that governs your problem. You assemble this body of authority by identifying *potentially* relevant primary authorities and evaluating them for relevance and validity. This phase is central to your research process. Like the other phases of the research process, this phase requires you to make numerous decisions, including whether to research in online or in print sources, how best to use secondary sources, what resources and processes to use to expand your research, and when to use a citator to validate a potentially relevant authority.

A. Questions to Ask as You Proceed

1. Which Resources and Techniques?

As you search for binding authority, you will encounter myriad resources. These resources are divided into four general categories: research gateways; sources of primary authority; sources of secondary authority; and citators[9] and finding tools. Research gateways provide access to primary and secondary authority and to citators and finding tools. Table 2-4 identifies some of the key resources you will encounter as a legal researcher. Later chapters discuss these resources in depth.

---

9. A citator tracks authority by citation and thus allows you to determine whether a specific legal authority remains valid. Specific ways to use citators to validate primary authority are addressed in the chapters relating to specific types of primary authority.

Table 2-4. Key Resources for Legal Research

Research Gateways	Primary Sources	Secondary Sources	Finding Tools & Citators
• Law library • Google Scholar • University legal information aggregators (e.g., Cornell, Washburn) • Commercial legal research services (e.g., Lexis Advance, Westlaw, Bloomberg Law)	• Constitutions • Statutes • Regulations • Cases • Municipal ordinances • Executive orders	• Treatises or hornbooks • Practice guides • Continuing legal education materials • Articles in legal periodicals • Restatements • ALR annotations • Legal encyclopedias	• Key number digests • Annotations to codes • *Shepard's* • KeyCite • BCite

Legal resources, from primary and secondary authorities to citators and finding tools, may have more than one function in a research process. Primary and secondary authorities form the basis of your substantive analysis of the law, but they cite other authority, so they also serve as finding tools. For example, cases cite to the authority underlying their reasoning, and thus lead you to additional primary authority. Codes arrange statutes[10] and regulations[11] topically, and thus help you find related statutes and regulations. Secondary sources,[12] including books and legal periodicals, cite primary and secondary authority to support their reasoning. Because of these citations, books and legal periodicals serve as finding tools as well as potentially persuasive authority. Other resources—for example, *American Law Reports* (ALR) annotations and legal encyclopedias—explain the law and so fall into the category of secondary sources. But these sources should ordinarily not be cited as legal authority because they function mainly as sources of background information and as finding tools but not as persuasive authority.[13]

Commercial services often provide extremely valuable research resources along with primary authority. For example, the West Key Number System[14]

---

10. Chapter 6 addresses statutory research, including how to update a statute to make sure it is the version currently in effect.

11. Chapter 8 discusses regulations.

12. Chapter 3 discusses secondary sources.

13. See Chapter 3 on the persuasiveness of different types of secondary authority.

14. Chapter 5 explains the West Key Number System.

uses summaries of points of law within cases ("headnotes") to organize cases according to a system of general topics and more specific key numbers. This system, which is available both in print and online, serves as an index to cases. Lexis Advance and Bloomberg Law also have headnote systems for topical case-law research. For statutes, commercial services publish "annotated codes," which present topical arrangements of statutes along with numerous tools for statutory research. In an annotated code, the text of a section of a statute is followed by references to amendments, citations to cases interpreting the section, and citations to relevant regulations and secondary sources. Commercial legal citators are essential resources for research because they help you validate authority by listing all the instances in which an authority has been cited. Citators also serve as finding tools because they cite authorities and thus lead to additional relevant authorities.

2. Print or Online?

Legal research materials are available in print and online, though not every resource is available in both. If your research project involves an area of law that is unfamiliar to you, you will likely begin by seeking background information and entry points by searching for a relevant secondary source through an online gateway—your law library's online catalog, a free internet resource such as Google Scholar or a legal research hub like Cornell's Legal Information Institute, or a commercial research service. You may then continue your research online or use your entry points in print sources. If you are familiar with the area of law you are researching, it may be more efficient to go directly to a print resource you have used in the past.

Many research tasks can be performed equally well in print or online, but for some tasks, for example, using a citator to validate authority or updating a statute, online sources are easier to use than print sources and provide more current information.[15] Thus, you should use online materials for these purposes.

3. How to Keep Track of Your Research?

In even an apparently simple research project, you will encounter many resources and use a number of techniques. To avoid duplicating your efforts, keep a record of where you have been and what you have done. Include a record of leads you decided not to follow; you might want to come back to them at some future point. In addition, keeping track of your research will contribute

---

15. As a general rule, online sources are more up-to-date because of the time required for printing and distributing updates in print.

to the success of your legal problem-solving process by promoting reflection on your research process and findings.

There is no set way to keep track of your research; the style and level of detail you use depends on the nature of the problem and on your personal preference. You might keep a word processing document called "Research Process—X Matter" and make detailed journal entries after every research session. You might also use tools provided by a commercial research service. Familiarize yourself with the tools Lexis Advance, Westlaw, and Bloomberg Law provide for reviewing your research history and saving documents. If you print out research result lists or photocopy print digest pages, annotate them so you can reconstruct your thought processes later.

B. Five Basic Tasks in the Search for Binding Authority

Although your research process may vary somewhat depending on the problem, assembling the body of relevant primary authority will involve at least the basic tasks set forth in Table 2-5.

Table 2-5. Five Basic Research Tasks

Task #1:	Find an entry point.
Task #2:	Use your entry point to assemble a preliminary list of authorities.
Task #3:	Analyze relevant authority in depth.
Task #4:	Expand your research to identify other relevant authorities.
Task #5:	Validate the authorities on which you plan to rely.

Task #1 and Task #2 are the first steps you will take. Task #3, Task #4, and Task #5 will occur at multiple points in your research process.

1. Task #1: Find an Entry Point

Today most legal researchers find an initial entry point through an online resource instead of through print finding tools. One of the main challenges a researcher faces in using online resources is how to deal with the sheer volume of material that results from a search. Commercial research services mitigate this challenge to some extent by letting you apply filters to your search, so, for example, you can narrow your search to a particular jurisdiction or type of material. Even when you apply filters to a search, reading a secondary source first can contribute substantially to an efficient and effective research process.

a. Finding an Entry Point through a Secondary Source

Secondary sources provide entry points because the authors of works about the law cite sources, both primary and secondary, for their assertions. These citations are entry points because they lead to other potentially relevant authority. When a search of an online database yields a result that includes both primary and secondary authority, a secondary source can help you work through the search result by pointing to the primary sources that are most relevant. In addition, the background information in the secondary source can help you refine your search queries.

A secondary source that is useful in Massachusetts legal research is the *Massachusetts Practice Series*, known among Massachusetts lawyers as "*Mass. Practice*."[16] This widely used "treatise" is really a series of monographs,[17] written by experts on a wide range of topics.[18] It is available in print and also in some online legal databases. If you were to pursue the potential consumer protection issue raised when Max Roberts was served food containing animal products in a restaurant that purported to be a vegan establishment, you might consult the title of *Mass. Practice* that focuses on Chapter 93A of the Massachusetts General Laws, which regulates business practices for consumer protection.[19] This title of *Mass. Practice* would give you background information as well as entry points for your search for binding authority through its references to primary authority, including to Chapter 93A and to cases interpreting the statute.

"Continuing legal education" (CLE) materials are also available in print and online, and they also provide background and entry points.[20] For example, if your project requires you to advise your non-profit client on how to apply for a state tax exemption, you might start your research with a 2014 publication by Massachusetts Continuing Legal Education entitled *Massachusetts Nonprofit Organizations*, which contains a chapter on qualifying for a tax exemption, with numerous references to primary authority.[21]

---

16. Chapter 3 discusses how to use this resource.

17. A monograph is a detailed treatment of a single subject.

18. *Mass. Practice* also provides helpful checklists and sample forms.

19. See Michael C. Gilleran, *The Law of Chapter 93A 2d* (*Massachusetts Practice Series*, Vol. 52, West 2007).

20. In addition to explaining the law and providing citations, continuing legal education materials may walk you through a transaction, for example, the sale of real estate or organizing a corporation, and provide sample forms.

21. *Massachusetts Nonprofit Organizations* vol. 1, ch. 3 (Mass. CLE 2014).

A general print treatise can provide an entry point, even if the treatise is not limited to Massachusetts law. For example, assume that you represent a client who last year sold for $25 at a yard sale a painting that both buyer and seller thought was of little value. Your client recently learned from a relative that beneath the top layer of paint is a very old painting worth a great deal of money. If your client had been aware of what was under the top layer of paint, she would not have sold the painting for $25, and she wants to know if she can get the painting back. To begin researching this problem, you might consult a hornbook,[22] for example, *Contracts* by E. Allen Farnsworth.[23] Perusing the Table of Contents, you find Chapter 9, entitled "Failure of a Basic Assumption: Mistake, Impracticability and Frustration," and beneath that § 9.2, "Types of Mistake." Although the text of the treatise does not address Massachusetts law specifically, it has a general discussion that provides background on this topic. A footnote citing a Massachusetts case provides an entry point into Massachusetts law.[24] You can also jump-start your research by using other secondary sources that are available in print and online, for example, an article in a legal periodical, a legal encyclopedia, or an ALR annotation.[25]

Secondary sources are helpful tools for finding entry points, but they may not always be the right tool for the specific job. Described below are some techniques for finding entry points when you do not have access to an appropriate secondary source.

b. Finding an Entry Point to an Annotated Code

If no reliable secondary source provides entry points for your research project, look for an entry point through a full-text search for a relevant provision of a constitution or a statute[26] in an online resource[27] or by using a print or

---

22. The term "hornbook" describes a treatise, generally in one volume, that is designed primarily for law students. In addition to Farnsworth, you may have encountered *Dobbs on Torts*, a popular hornbook. Chapter 3 addresses hornbooks in greater detail.

23. E. Allen Farnsworth, *Contracts* (4th ed., Aspen Publishers 2004).

24. *Id.* at 602 n. 5.

25. See Chapter 3 on how to use these resources.

26. Constitutions and statutes are above cases in the hierarchy of primary authority, so you should seek a relevant provision of a constitution or statute before turning to case law research.

27. Appendix B addresses the basics for constructing a full-text search. Ordinarily, annotated codes are available online only through commercial research services. But a free search engine may provide a link to a statute and thus an entry point to a print annotated code that is available in a library.

online index to an annotated code.[28] To use an index, generate search terms by asking yourself questions about the problem using one of the techniques discussed earlier in this chapter.[29] Then, look up the search terms in the index. You may not get a direct hit on the first try. In that situation, use a different search term and rely on cross-references within the index to help you identify a potentially relevant provision of a constitution or section of a statute. Whether you use a print or online resource, once you have an entry point to an annotated code, you are in a position to expand your research by using the table of contents to the relevant chapter or title to lead you to related sections; following up cross-references in statutory sections; and using editorial enhancements to lead you to relevant regulations, cases, and secondary authority.

c. Finding an Entry Point to Case Law through a Subject Search or a Full-Text Search

If you are satisfied that there is no controlling constitutional provision or statute or helpful secondary source, seek an entry point into relevant case law through a subject search in print or online or through a full-text search in an online resource. When you search by subject, you are searching for relevant judicial opinions in a manner similar to the way you would search an index. When you conduct a full-text search, you are searching for occurrences of specific language within judicial opinions.

Lexis Advance lets you search by subject using the "Search by Topic" feature. Similarly, Bloomberg Law lets you search cases by subject using the BNA Headnotes and Classification Outlines tool. The Lexis Advance and Bloomberg Law tools are available only online.[30] The West Key Number System is available in print, through the American Digest System, or online, through Westlaw.[31]

You may also locate an entry point by finding relevant cases through a full-text search in an online database. Most commercial research services let you construct a full-text search using specialized terms and connectors;[32] they also let you conduct a natural-language search.[33] At this early stage in your research,

---

28. Chapter 6 discusses how to use annotated codes in print and online.
29. See Tables 2-1 and 2-2 and accompanying text.
30. See Chapter 5 for a more detailed discussion of these features.
31. Chapter 5 describes the Key Number System and how to use it in print and online.
32. See Chapter 5 for a discussion of terms-and-connectors searching in a case law search.
33. See Chapter 5 for a discussion of natural-language searching in a case law search.

you are unlikely to be familiar with the precise syntax the courts use in the area you are researching. Thus, at this stage it is generally more efficient to use natural-language searching because it does not assume familiarity with the court's language and syntax. Terms-and-connectors searching, a more precise but less flexible type of full-text search, may be useful when you are more familiar with court's language and syntax.[34]

2. Task #2: Use Your Entry Point to Assemble a Preliminary List of Authorities

Once you find an entry point, use it to assemble a preliminary list of authorities — those authorities that are potentially relevant to your problem. Although you may be tempted to gather a great deal of potentially relevant material and then evaluate it all at once, this strategy is generally not efficient for legal research. Legal research is a reflective process: you can learn something from every step, even if it is a misstep, and integrating what you learn into what you already know helps you fine-tune your research. Analyzing material as you develop your preliminary list of authorities will contribute to the effectiveness and efficiency of your research process. This analysis will help ground you in the area of law you are researching as well as help you gauge the success of your research strategy thus far. In addition, your analysis of the law at this point may suggest the need for additional factual research.

How you develop your preliminary list depends on your entry point and the resources you use. For example, if your entry point is a secondary source that purports to cover comprehensively the area you are researching, like the Massachusetts Continuing Legal Education publication relating to non-profits described earlier in this chapter, it may gather most of the relevant primary authorities and thus create your preliminary list. When you have this type of resource, your subsequent research tasks will mainly involve following up on the sources to which it cites.[35]

---

34. Appendix B is a guide to the basics of constructing a full-text search on Lexis Advance, Westlaw, or Bloomberg Law.

35. But even if a secondary source seems comprehensive, you are not entitled to rely completely on the research and conclusions of the author. Rather, you must read and analyze every primary authority on which you rely. Moreover, you must always question the comprehensiveness of the secondary source. Bringing your insight to bear on the problem may suggest lines of research that the author of the secondary source did not consider. Finally, you always need to expand your research to make sure it is comprehensive and update your research to make sure you are relying only on valid authorities.

If your entry point is the citation to a statute from a secondary source, an index search, or a full-text search, consider using an annotated code to assemble your preliminary list of authorities. First, make sure you have the most up-to-date version of the statute.[36] Then, familiarize yourself with the language of the statute and what it provides on its face. If the statute cross-references other sections, look them up and read them as well, first making sure that the version of each cross-referenced section is up to date. Then, to assemble your preliminary list of authorities, consult the table of contents of the title or chapter of the code that includes your statute to identify related sections, including sections setting forth definitions. Use the annotations to the statute to point you to regulations, to cases interpreting the statute, and to secondary sources.[37]

Annotated codes have tools to help you sort research results for your preliminary list. An annotated code may refer you to too many cases to allow you to read each one carefully. Thus, you will have to do some preliminary sorting. The annotated code helps you in two ways: first, it gives summaries of cases rather than simply citations, and second, when a given code section has a lot of case annotations, they are generally indexed. The index to the annotations and case summaries help direct your focus to cases that are most relevant to your problem. Case summaries in annotated codes are helpful in other ways. By identifying the court that decided the case and the year it was decided, a case summary informs you about the weight of the decision. A decision of a higher court is more authoritative than a decision of a lower court, so as you make your first cut through the material, look at decisions of higher courts first. A more recent case will present a more current take on the law than an older case. Figure 2-1 shows case summaries following the text of Mass. Gen. Laws ch. 93A, §9 in the annotated Massachusetts code on Lexis Advance.

When your entry point is a case that you have located through a secondary source, a subject search, a full-text search, or an annotated code, read the case and use your analysis of the case to help you sift through the rest of the results of your search or to craft a more effective search. Compare citations within your case with your other search results. If your search missed a number of cases that your case cites, you may need to revise your search. Use the citation of your case in a legal citator—*Shepard's Citations* of Lexis Advance, Westlaw's

---

36. Statues may be amended, so updating is crucial. Chapter 6 discusses updating statutes in print and online.

37. Annotated codes do not include every possibly relevant reference. Thus, after you use the annotated code to assemble a group of relevant authorities, you must expand your research to include authorities not cited in the annotations.

Figure 2-1. Case Summaries in Annotated Code on Lexis Advance

꙳ 3. −Retroactivity

ALM GL c 93A is not to be given retroactive application to practices engaged in prior to its enactment. Gopen v. American Supply Co. (Mass. App. Ct. 1980), 10 Mass. App. Ct. 342, 407 N.E.2d 1255, 1980 Mass. App. LEXIS 1265.

ALM GL c 93A, § 11, enacted by Acts 1972, ch. 614, § 2, giving businessmen right of action under ALM GL c 93A, was not retroactively applicable to claims based on activities which occurred from 1966 through 1970. Evans v. Multicon Constr. Corp. (Mass. App. Ct. 1991), 30 Mass. App. Ct. 728, 574 N.E.2d 395, 1991 Mass. App. LEXIS 418.

When a Massachusetts supplier contracted to design and supply an automotive part to a Michigan manufacturer, which allegedly obtained the part from another source, and the supplier then sued the manufacturer for deceptive practices under ALM GL c 93A, § 11, which required that the alleged deceptive practices occurred primarily and substantially within Massachusetts, given the liberality with which notice pleadings were received and the court's authority, under Mass. R. Civ. P. 8(c), to treat the manufacturer's pleadings as if they properly raised the affirmative defense that the acts complained of did not primarily occur in Massachusetts, the manufacturer did not waive this affirmative defense. Stoneridge Control Devices, Inc. v. Teleflex, Inc. (Mass. Super. Ct. 2004), 17 Mass. L. Rep. 335, 2004 Mass. Super. LEXIS 23.

꙳ 4. Who may sue

ABCC has no power to prosecute civil actions for damages or to seek injunctive relief or to institute criminal proceedings under ALM GL c 93 or ALM GL c 93A on behalf of persons aggrieved by violations of alcoholic beverages control law. J. & J. Enterprises, Inc. v. Martignetti (Mass. 1976), 369 Mass. 535, 341 N.E.2d 645, 1976 Mass. LEXIS 859.

Standing requirement of ALM GL c 93A, § 11 is that plaintiff must be person who engages in conduct of any trade or commerce; thus city which took assignment of hospital patients' health insurance claims had standing to assert ALM GL c 93A claims against insurers. City of Boston v. Aetna Life Ins. Co. (Mass. 1987), 399 Mass. 569, 506 N.E.2d 106, 1987 Mass. LEXIS 1219.

Plaintiff must be person engaged in "trade or commerce" in order to have standing to assert claim under ALM GL c 93A, § 11. Clean Harbors of Braintree, Inc. v. Board of Health (Mass. 1991), 409 Mass. 834, 570 N.E.2d 987, 1991 Mass. LEXIS 197.

Town board of health was not engaged in trade or commerce and could not bring action under ALM GL c 93A, § 11 against operator of hazardous waste treatment and storage facility for operating without site assignment. Clean Harbors of Braintree, Inc. v. Board of Health (Mass. 1991), 409 Mass. 834, 570 N.E.2d 987, 1991 Mass. LEXIS 197.

Used with permission of LexisNexis.

KeyCite, or Bloomberg Law's BCite — to augment your preliminary list with cases decided after your case.[38]

As you assemble your preliminary list, you will ordinarily not be able to read thoroughly every case you encounter. Skim cases and use the case descriptions provided in a result list or an annotated code to help you decide which cases to include in your list. Although you should not base final judgments on skimming or reading case descriptions, remember that at this point

---

38. Citators provide lists of all authorities that cite a given piece of authority. Citators are discussed later in this chapter.

you are doing preliminary sorting and that legal resources are interconnected. Thus, it is likely that, if at this point you reject an authority that turns out to be important, it will resurface at a later point in your research process.[39] And the more practice you get in legal research, the more confidence you will gain in your ability to sort materials for relevance.

3. Task #3: Analyze Relevant Authority in Depth

After you assemble your preliminary list of authorities, look more closely at the authorities on the list to identify the authorities that are most relevant to your problem. Analyze these authorities in depth. These authorities are the law that applies to your client's problem, so deep analysis, not skimming, is the appropriate way to interact with the material. But even after you identify what you think is the core group of relevant authorities, always keep your mind open to new avenues of research your analysis may suggest.

4. Task #4: Expand Your Research

At some point in your research process, when you are confident that you have located a core group of relevant authorities, you will need to expand your research to make sure that your research is comprehensive. Like evaluating your findings, expanding your research is not a discrete step in a research process, but an operation that occurs frequently, as you go along. For example, you can use a statute to locate additional relevant authorities by using the table of contents, editorial enhancements following the text of the statute in an annotated code, and a citator, which would lead you to authorities citing the statute. To use a case to expand your research, mine the case for authorities the case cites and use the case to get access to other cases with the same Lexis Advance headnotes or West topics and key numbers. You can also use a citator to expand your research by locating authorities that cite cases that are central to your analysis.

5. Task #5: Validate Your Research

As with other research tasks, validating your results is not something to put off to the end of your research process. If you do put it off, you might discover that you based your analysis on a case that was overruled, significantly limited, or superseded by statute or that you relied on a statute that was amended or repealed. Thus, use a citator to validate your research at key points in your research process to ensure that the main authorities on which you propose to

---

39. See discussion near the end of this chapter on "triangulating" your research.

rely are valid. At or toward the end of your research, use a citator to validate every authority on which you rely.

A citator is a tool that lets you look up the citation to a legal authority and see a list of all the authorities that cite it. This central feature of citators makes them essential tools to validate most forms of primary legal authority. Introduced in 1873, *Shepard's Citations* was the citator used almost universally by lawyers until Westlaw introduced KeyCite in 1997. Lexis Advance has a popular online version of *Shepard's*. While *Shepard's* continues to be available in print, many law libraries no longer maintain it because it is cumbersome to use, less current than online citators, and expensive to maintain. Most researchers therefore validate authorities using *Shepard's* online or KeyCite. In the 2000s, Bloomberg Law introduced its own citator, BCite.[40]

Shepard's online, KeyCite, and BCite use symbols to indicate whether an authority's validity has been compromised. For example, *Shepard's* uses a yellow triangle to indicate that a case has had possible negative treatment. Figure 2-2 shows some of the symbols *Shepard's* uses to convey information concerning the validity of a case. Figure 2-3 shows some of the symbols KeyCite uses. And Figure 2-4 shows some of BCite's symbols.

Figure 2-2. *Shepard's* Symbols

Shepard's signal indicators

Checking Citations in Shepard's

Once you have Shepardized a case, one of the following symbols will appear in the upper left of the screen next to the case citation.

Note:
Not every case will have a *Shepard's* Signal indicators.

* Signal Legend:
- Warning: Negative treatment is indicated
- Warning: Negative case treatment is indicated for statute
- Questioned: validity questioned by citing refs
- Caution: Possible negative treatment
- Positive treatment is indicated
- Citing Refs. With Analysis Available
- Citation information available

If one of the first three Symbols appears for your case, review the negative treatment to verify that your particular point of law is still good.

Used with permission of LexisNexis.

---

40. Other online research services provide citators, but these are generally not as robust as *Shepard's*, KeyCite, or BCite.

Figure 2-3. KeyCite Symbols

KeyCite®

KeyCite is the powerful citation research service available exclusively on Westlaw and WestlawNext. Use KeyCite at every step of your research to help you find, understand, and update the law.

The KeyCite citation network is integrated with the West Key Number system. This integration allows KeyCite to connect documents that discuss the same legal issues with the analytical materials that explain those issues.

Once you have found a document upon which to base your legal argument, KeyCite Flags alert you to negative references or events that may impact the validity of that document.

- A yellow flag indicates a document has some negative treatment.
- A red flag indicates a document is no longer good law for at least one point of law.
- A blue-striped flag indicates a document has been appealed to the U.S. Courts of Appeals or the U.S. Supreme Court (excluding appeals originating from agencies).

KeyCite citing references help you investigate how other authorities have interpreted that document. If your document is a court decision, KeyCite History tells you if that decision was reversed or upheld in a later appeal.

For more information on using KeyCite, please see the KeyCite tutorial in the Help Center.

Used with permission of Thomson Reuters.

Figure 2-4. BCite Symbols

Composite Analysis

The Composite Analysis is a visual representation of the Direct History and Case Analysis portions of BCite, displaying the overall status of the case.

Composite	Definition	Indicator
Positive	This composite results from the Case Analysis. One or more courts cite to, discuss, or follow this opinion with approval.	✚
No Citing Cases	This composite results from the Case Analysis. No courts have cited to this opinion.	✚
Distinguished	This composite results from the Case Analysis. One or more courts differentiate this opinion on the law or the facts.	✏
Caution	This composite results from either the Direct History or Case Analysis. If the Caution composite results from the Direct History, the opinion has been modified, clarified, or amended by a subsequent decision within the Direct History. If the Caution composite results from the Case Analysis, one or more courts have criticized the legal reasoning of the opinion without overruling it.	⚠
Superseded by Statute	This composite results from the Case Analysis. One or more courts state that this opinion has been superseded, displaced or rendered obsolete by an intervening statute, rule or regulation.	⬚
Negative	This composite results from either the Direct History or Case Analysis. If the Negative composite results from the Direct History, the opinion has been reversed, vacated, or depublished in full or in part by a subsequent decision within the Direct History. If the Negative composite results from the Case Analysis, one or more courts have overruled the opinion in full or in part, or stated that the opinion has been overruled in full or in part by a previous decision.	⬛

Reproduced with permission from Bloomberg Law. Copyright 2016 by The Bureau of National Affairs, Inc. (800-372-1033) <http://www.bna.com>.

IV. Third Phase: Wrapping Up Your Research

How do you know when to stop researching? Like so many questions relating to legal research, the answer to this question is, "It depends." Mainly, it depends on your analysis of the authorities you have found and how confident you are in this analysis as the basis for your problem solving. If your research leaves you with a big question, continue researching until you find an answer—or until you satisfy yourself that the authorities do not answer your question.

You can increase your confidence that you have not missed an important line of authorities by "triangulating" your research. You can accomplish this check on your work by redoing parts of your research using methods different from the main method you used initially. Assume you used as an entry point the citation to a case you found in a secondary source, and then moved forward by using it to build a subject search. You might double-check your research with a full-text search in an online database. You could also double-check your research by using a citator to identify all the authorities that cited the case. If you use at least two different methods[41] and the same authorities keep coming up, you can feel fairly confident that you have identified the authorities that are significant for your problem. Analogously, assume that you used the annotations to a section of a statute to locate regulations promulgated under it and cases interpreting it. Consider using a citator to identify all the authorities that cite the statute or running a full-text search.

If you use more than one method to perform Task #4, expanding your research, you may not need to double-check your research. Whether you do will depend on how your understanding of the problem developed as you did your research. If, as you researched, you followed many and varied paths, this is a good time to redo key parts of your research, using a different method, to review your overall research process. If your research proceeded pretty much along the lines you envisioned as you oriented yourself to the problem, then you probably do not need at this point to redo research tasks you already performed. Rather, use this phase as an opportunity to reflect on your research process to make sure you are confident that you are ready to stop.

---

41. For example, a method based on word searching is "different" from a method based on index searching. Subject searching and using a citator are still other "different" methods.

Chapter 3

Secondary Sources

I. Introduction

Secondary sources are important resources for the legal researcher. Although secondary sources are never binding authority,[1] they help the legal researcher in three ways. First, discussions of law in secondary sources may help you understand the law relevant to your client's problem. Second, citations to primary authority in secondary sources provide entry points in your search for primary authority. Finally, analysis in secondary sources may be persuasive authority when there is little or no primary authority on point.

Legal researchers encounter many types of secondary sources. This chapter introduces legal books, including academic treatises and works intended for the practitioner; legal periodicals, including law reviews, bar journals, and legal newspapers; websites and blogs; continuing legal education (CLE) publications; encyclopedias; restatements, uniform laws, and model acts; forms; and jury instructions. It also introduces two hybrid sources of secondary and primary authority: *American Law Reports* (ALR), which reports cases as well as provides commentary on subject areas, and topical services (also called "loose-leaf services"), publications that collate primary and secondary authority relevant to an area of law.

Depending on your research project and on the nature of a given secondary source, you may use a secondary source as persuasive authority, as a source of background analysis, or as a finding tool. A secondary source written by a recognized expert is citable as persuasive authority; other secondary sources may

---

1. A secondary source, by definition, is not "law" because it is not an official statement of a government unit. For a more detailed discussion of this point, see Chapter 1 on authority.

be citable as well.[2] To determine whether a secondary source is citable, consider the type and author of the secondary source. In general, you should not cite continuing legal education material, ALR annotations, or legal encyclopedias. When you use a secondary source for insight into the analysis of a problem, do not rely on it automatically. Go behind the secondary source to read primary authorities on which the secondary source bases its analysis so you can evaluate the secondary source for yourself.

Although some secondary sources are available only in print, many secondary sources are available electronically from the publisher, and some are also available on services such as Lexis Advance, Westlaw, Bloomberg Law, and HeinOnline.[3] Some secondary sources are available only online.

II. Books

A. Books in General

Books, including treatises, practice guides, and hornbooks, are useful secondary sources. Generally, a book that is called a "treatise" is a comprehensive treatment of an area of law by a recognized scholar.[4] A hornbook is a condensed treatment of an area, intended primarily for law students, which may or may not be written by a recognized scholar.[5] Books in the *Nutshell* series[6] are even more condensed treatments that are particularly helpful to students as course companions or as introductions to fields of law.

Some books that focus on the needs of the practitioner may be called treatises, but may also be called practice guides. For example, *Massachusetts Practice Series*, a collection of monographs on areas of Massachusetts law, is referred

---

2. Although a book or article by a recognized expert is ordinarily more persuasive than a student note, a well-crafted student note that is right on point may be more persuasive than a tangential article by an expert.

3. A secondary source may be available only on one of these services. Thus, the decision to subscribe to one or another commercial service may be determined by whether the service includes that secondary source.

4. *See, e.g.*, Richard J. Pierce, *Administrative Law Treatise* (5th ed., Aspen Publishers 2010).

5. West, LexisNexis, Wolters Kluwer, and other publishers publish books that are intended for students on a wide range of topics.

6. *Nutshells* are published by West. Titles in the *Nutshell* series include *Contracts in a Nutshell, Torts in a Nutshell, Regulated Industries in a Nutshell, Legal Drafting in a Nutshell*, and many others.

to as a treatise, as a practice guide, and even sometimes as an encyclopedia.[7] Similarly, *Handbook of Massachusetts Evidence* may be referred to as a treatise or as a practice guide. These distinctions in terminology are not really important to your work with secondary sources. What is important is the functional distinction: How can a given source help you in your research project? Figure 3-1 shows an excerpt from *Handbook of Massachusetts Evidence*.

Figure 3-1. Excerpt from *Handbook of Massachusetts Evidence*

§ 8.25   The Catchall Exception

Fed R Evid 807 provides a catchall exception not included as part of the Proposed Massachusetts Rules of Evidence:

Residual Exception

A statement not specifically covered by Rule 803 or 804 but having equivalent circumstantial guarantees of trustworthiness, is not excluded by the hearsay rule, if the court determines that (A) the statement is offered as evidence of a material fact; (B) the statement is more probative on the point for which it is offered than any other evidence which the proponent can procure through reasonable efforts; and (C) the general purposes of these rules and the interests of justice will best be served by the admission of the statement into evidence. However, a statement may not be admitted under this exception unless the proponent of it makes

---

Mary, 414 Mass 705, 610 NE2d 898 (1993); *Adoption of Sean*, 36 Mass App 261, 630 NE2d 604 (1994) (guardian ad litem reports containing hearsay are admissible in proceedings to dispense with consent for adoption under GL 215, § 56A); *Adoption of Arthur*, 34 Mass App 914, 609 NE2d 486 (1993) (same); *Adoption of Kenneth*, 31 Mass App 946, 580 NE2d 392 (1991); *Custody of Tracy*, 31 Mass App 481, 579 NE2d 1362 (1991).
    [16] *Adoption of Georgia*, 433 Mass 62, 739 NE2d 694 (2000); *Guardianship of Pollard*, 54 Mass App 318, 764 NE2d 935 (2002).

Source: Mark S. Brodin & Michael Avery, *Handbook of Massachusetts Evidence 2016 Edition* (Wolters Kluwer 2015). Reprinted with permission of Wolters Kluwer Legal and Regulatory Solutions U.S.

Like other secondary sources, books are useful in legal research because they discuss legal topics, often in depth, and cite authority for their discussions. If you are unfamiliar with an area of law, the discussion of that area in a book

---

7. *Massachusetts Practice Series* is published by West. It is available in print and online through Westlaw.

may give you a helpful introduction. If you are somewhat familiar with the area, the discussion may deepen your understanding. Books cite authority for their assertions and thus provide entry points to the body of primary authority that governs your problem.[8] Some books that focus on the needs of the practitioner provide checklists or forms that serve as starting points for drafting documents.[9]

As with other secondary sources, some books are available only in print,[10] while others are available both in print and online—on Lexis Advance, Westlaw, Bloomberg Law, HeinOnline, or by subscription directly from the publisher.[11] Still others are available only online.[12]

In addition to being available in one or more formats, books are updated in a variety of ways to reflect changes in the law or provide additional authority. In print, some books are published in bound volumes and are updated by "pocket parts"—updating pages inserted in a "pocket" in the back of a bound volume—or separate annual supplements and subsequent editions. Other books, published in loose-leaf binders, are updated by replacing outdated pages throughout the binder with current material. When published online, a book may be continuously updated or you may need to refer to a separate electronic supplement.

To locate a book in print when you do not know its exact title, run a keyword search in your law library's catalog using words related to the general topic you are researching. For a well-known treatise, include the name of the author as a search term. When searching for practice-oriented material, use the name of the publisher (for example, Massachusetts Continuing Legal Education). After locating one relevant book on your library shelves, browse the titles shelved around it for additional resources.

To use a print book, look up your research terms in the table of contents or the index, which is generally in the last volume of the series. The index

---

8. See Chapter 2 for a general discussion of how secondary sources figure in a research process.

9. Many titles within *Massachusetts Practice Series* include forms and checklists.

10. For example, Pierce's *Administrative Law Treatise* and *Handbook of Massachusetts Evidence* are currently available only in print.

11. As examples, *Nimmer on Copyright* is available online on Lexis Advance but not on Westlaw, while *McCarthy on Trademark* is available online on Westlaw but not on Lexis Advance.

12. This applies to serials that are no longer printed in hard copy, for example, the Environmental Law Institute's *Environmental Law Reporter*, available to subscribers at www.elr.info. Bloomberg BNA has topical services that are available only online.

may refer you to a page number, section number, or paragraph number. Then, follow the reference to material in the book that is relevant to your research project.

Lexis Advance, Westlaw, and Bloomberg Law let you search for a book through a full-text search or by browsing for a source. In Lexis Advance, you can use the "Browse" menu to search for a specific source, or, still within the Browse menu, narrow your search for a source by category, jurisdiction, practice area, and publisher. Similarly, in Westlaw you can browse for a particular type of material from a particular jurisdiction on a particular topic or use the search bar within the Browse feature to locate a specific source. Bloomberg Law has a more limited range of books than Lexis Advance or Westlaw, but has a very wide range of topical services—practice-oriented publications discussed later in this chapter—provided through Bloomberg BNA. You can locate these and other secondary sources through the Browse menu or through a full-text search. To use the Browse menu to find Massachusetts-specific secondary sources on Bloomberg Law, go to "State Law and Regulations," select Massachusetts from the map of the United States, and then select "Mass. secondary sources."

Always check whether the commercial research service you are using permits you to search a book's index or browse a table of contents. For many research projects, these methods are more efficient than full-text searching. Also, even an experienced researcher will benefit from clicking on the information icon (often the letter "i") that applies to a source. This leads to general information about the source, including how recently it was updated and tips for using it.

B. Massachusetts-Specific Books

Numerous books address Massachusetts law specifically.[13] One of the most helpful Massachusetts-specific secondary sources is *Massachusetts Practice Series*, commonly referred to as "*Mass. Practice*," a multi-volume set written by judges, law professors, and experienced lawyers. *Mass. Practice* is available in bound volumes in print and on Westlaw. Among the titles in the series are *Administrative Law and Practice*, *Consumer Law*, *Criminal Law*, *Evidence*, *Estate Planning*, *Family Law and Practice*, *Landlord and Tenant Law*, *Mental Health Law*, *Probate Law and Practice*, *Summary of Basic Law*, *Taxation*, and

---

13. For a list of Massachusetts-specific books, see *Handbook of Legal Research in Massachusetts* § 11.4 (Mary Ann Neary & Ruth G. Matz eds., 3d ed., Mass. CLE 2009 & Supps. 2012 & 2015).

Tort Law. In addition to commentary on the law and citations to authority, many titles in the series include forms that are helpful starting points for drafting documents.

To search *Mass. Practice* in print, use the general index to the series or use the table of contents or index to an individual title. On Westlaw, browse the table of contents[14] of the series or, within the Browse feature, use full-text searching in the database of an individual title or for the series as a whole. You can also use the global search box and narrow your search to "Mass. Practice." As with many secondary sources, using an index or browsing the table of contents of *Mass. Practice* may be more efficient than conducting a full-text search.

III. Legal Periodicals

A. Overview

Law reviews and law journals publish scholarly articles written by law professors, judges, practitioners, and students, while bar journals publish articles with a practitioner's focus. Legal newspapers publish legal news, including some court decisions and disciplinary proceedings, as well as analysis of legal developments.

B. Academic Law Reviews and Law Journals

1. Law Reviews in General

Articles in academic law reviews and law journals generally discuss, often in great detail, a specific legal issue. Freed from the constraints of representing clients, authors explore a wide range of topics, including whether the laws currently in force are the best legal rules or how they should change.

Articles published in academic law reviews and journals help you understand current law because authors generally explain existing law to provide foundation for their arguments. Articles may identify trends in the law, and this information can help you analyze your client's problem. The many citations in these articles provide entry points to further research.

Unlike the literature of other professions, law reviews and law journals are generally edited and published by law students. Most of these periodicals cover a broad range of topics. A growing number of student-edited journals focus

---

14. The table of contents appears as the first screen when you gain access to *Mass. Practice* through the Browse feature.

on a specific area of law, for example, *Drake Journal of Agriculture Law* and *Boston College Environmental Affairs Law Review*. Each of the nine Massachusetts law schools publishes at least one law review or journal; some publish several.[15]

Law reviews generally include articles by recognized experts as well as by students. Articles by students, which are called "Notes" or "Comments," are ordinarily not as authoritative as articles written by experts. Nonetheless, the analysis in a student article may be helpful. "Case Notes" or "Recent Developments" are shorter pieces by students that summarize developments in the law. Footnotes in student pieces may provide useful entry points for research.

Other law journals are "peer edited," meaning that non-students, generally law professors, select and edit the articles to be published. An example of this type of law journal is *Law and Contemporary Problems*, a faculty-edited publication of Duke Law School.

While some legal periodicals are published only electronically,[16] most continue to be published in print. The trend, however, is for law libraries to cancel subscriptions to legal periodicals that are easily accessible online.[17]

In print, periodicals are published first in soft-cover booklets. Later, several issues may be bound into a single volume. Articles are cited by volume number, the name of the journal, and the first page of the article.

Online, articles are still referenced by the print volume, journal name, and page. Articles may be available without charge on the internet or through a commercial research service. Lexis Advance, Westlaw, and Bloomberg Law do not have comprehensive coverage of law review articles. A service may be selective in the law reviews it includes and, for many law reviews, it may not cover issues very far back in time. To determine how far back a service covers a given law review, click on the information icon for the law review.

HeinOnline is an important legal research resource that provides access to PDF versions of a wide range of legal materials. HeinOnline includes a large

---

15. For a list of legal periodicals published in Massachusetts, see *Handbook of Legal Research in Massachusetts* § 11.1 (Mary Ann Neary & Ruth G. Matz eds., 3d ed., Mass. CLE 2009 & Supps. 2012 & 2015).

16. Examples are Boston College's *Intellectual Property and Technology Forum* at http://bciptf.org and the *Harvard International Law Review Online*, a companion to the print *Harvard International Law Review*, at www.harvardilj.org.

17. *See* Julian Aiken et al., "Not Your Parents' Law Library," 16 *Green Bag* 2d 13, 14 (2012).

number of legal periodicals going back, in many instances, to the first volume published. Although HeinOnline offers full-text searching, its search engine is not as sophisticated as those of Lexis Advance, Westlaw, or Bloomberg Law. Nonetheless, HeinOnline is a valuable resource, especially for the researcher who requires an article that is not included in one of the other legal commercial research services. Subscribers gain access to HeinOnline at www.heinonline.org or through their law library's website.

Shepard's and KeyCite cover some legal periodicals. Thus, you may be able to find out whether and how an article has been cited by another source.[18] Currently, Bloomberg Law's BCite does not include law review citations.

2. Locating Relevant Articles

To locate a relevant article you may use full-text searching of an online database or an index in print or online. Your choice of search method will depend on factors including how comprehensive your search needs to be. Generally, an index search will be more comprehensive than a full-text search, in part because of the nature of the databases being searched.

A full-text Google Scholar search may lead you to relevant articles, but there is no directory of the law reviews Google Scholar searches. The Law Practice Division of the American Bar Association has a search engine that searches the free full text of 400 law reviews.[19] These law reviews are listed on the website. You can also conduct a full-text search of law review article databases on commercial research services. Commercial research services identify the law reviews they cover.

Periodical indexes offer a way to locate relevant articles that is more comprehensive and may be more efficient than full-text searches. Indexes cover more periodicals than do the full-text databases of Lexis Advance, Westlaw, and Bloomberg Law. In index searching, subject headings that indicate what an article is primarily about help you search efficiently.

Today, many law libraries do not maintain updated periodical indexes in print. Most law libraries subscribe to one or both of two online versions of print indexes: *LegalTrac*[20] and *Index to Legal Periodicals and Books* (ILPB).

---

18. Citators are introduced in Chapter 2. Some legal periodicals are not covered by citators.

19. The URL for this website is americanbar.org/groups/departments_offices/legal_technology_resources/resources/free_journal_search.html.

20. In print, *LegalTrac* is known as *Current Law Index*. When it is accessed from another vendor, for example, Lexis or Westlaw, it is known as *Legal Resource Index*.

LegalTrac indexes articles going back to 1980, and ILPB has an online product that indexes articles going back to 1908. Lexis Advance and Westlaw both have an index called *Legal Resource Index*, which goes back to 1980. To locate *Legal Resource Index* on Lexis Advance, go to the Browse menu and type the name of the index in the "Search for a Source" box. To locate *Legal Resource Index* on Westlaw, browse to secondary sources and you will find a link to the index under "Tools and Resources." Currently, Bloomberg Law does not have a periodical index.

When you use a periodical index in Lexis Advance or Westlaw, you are not searching the full text of the article; you are only searching the title, author, and subject fields. If Lexis Advance or Westlaw includes the law review, the index entry will provide a link to the text of the article.

C. Bar Journals, Legal Newspapers, Blogs, and Websites

Bar journals publish articles of particular interest to attorneys practicing in a given state. Articles in bar journals tend to be shorter than articles published in law reviews and generally do not have as extensive footnotes. Moreover, bar journal articles have a practitioner's focus. Most bar journals publish articles on trends in law practice and firm management as well as articles analyzing recent developments in the law.

The American Bar Association publishes the *ABA Journal*, which has articles of general interest to attorneys across the nation. Two Massachusetts bar journals have statewide distribution: *Massachusetts Law Review* and *Boston Bar Journal*.

Periodical indexes cover most bar journals, and HeinOnline has an extensive collection. When you use a commercial service, check whether it includes the bar journal you are seeking. For example, Westlaw includes both *Massachusetts Law Review* and *Boston Bar Journal*, while Lexis Advance does not include *Massachusetts Law Review*. Bloomberg Law currently includes neither bar journal.

The leading legal newspaper in Massachusetts is *Massachusetts Lawyers Weekly*. It reports decisions issued by state and federal courts in Massachusetts; decisions of state agencies; changes to court rules; verdict and settlement reports; bar-discipline notices; and other legal news. The print version of *Mas-*

Both Lexis Advance and Westlaw allow you to access that database—and anything else you know the title of—by typing the title into the main search box.

sachusetts Lawyers Weekly is widely available in law libraries in Massachusetts. The online version is available only to subscribers.

Law firm websites and blogs written by Massachusetts lawyers provide analysis of legal developments and citations to primary and secondary authority. This material provides research entry points, but since the analysis presented on these websites and blogs may be geared to the specific interests of the authors' clients, be especially careful to evaluate for yourself the primary authority on which the analysis relies.

Organizations of lawyers who practice in specific areas maintain websites providing analysis and links to primary sources. Ordinarily, these professional organizations limit access to information on their websites to members of the organization. Figure 3-2 shows resources available on the website of the American Immigration Lawyers Association.

Figure 3-2. Website of American Immigration Lawyers Association

Source: www.aila.org.

IV. Topical ("Loose-Leaf") Services

A topical service is a comprehensive, hybrid source that combines primary and secondary material under one title. In areas of law like taxation and environmental law, a single title may contain statutes, administrative regulations, annotations to cases and agency opinions, and commentary. The benefit is obvious: all the material is gathered together so that the researcher does not have to consult multiple sources.

A. Print Resources

A topical service published in print is often referred to as a "loose-leaf" service because its pages are kept in loose-leaf notebooks instead of being bound as books. A loose-leaf service generally fills several volumes. The volumes may be arranged by topic, statute, or another system.

The loose-leaf format allows the publisher to send updates frequently; the subscriber removes outdated pages and inserts new pages on a regular basis. Because of this ability to update, print loose-leaf services were extremely popular with practicing lawyers before the advent of online resources. Because loose-leafs are so easy to use, many lawyers prefer to use topical services in print when they remain available in that format.

Before you look for substantive material in a looseleaf, review the "How to Use" section near the beginning of the first volume. Also consider skimming through a few volumes to become familiar with the organization of that particular service. Pay careful attention to each service's method and frequency of updating.

When you do not know the specific section of a loose-leaf that you need to consult, begin with the topical index. Often this is the first or last volume of the series. Look up your research terms and write down the reference numbers given. These will likely be paragraph numbers rather than page numbers. To maintain indexing despite frequent updates, loose-leaf services may be indexed by paragraph number. A "paragraph" may be just a few sentences, several actual paragraphs, or many pages in length. Even though page numbers may change with updates, paragraph references remain constant.

Turn to each paragraph number referenced in the index under your key terms. Realize that the paragraph number may be for the statute, regulations, annotations, or commentary. Turn to earlier and later pages around that paragraph number to ensure that you have reviewed all relevant material.

B. Online Topical Services

While libraries continue to maintain some loose-leafs in print, topical services are increasingly available online directly from the publisher or on Lexis Advance or Westlaw. Bloomberg BNA provides access on Bloomberg Law to a wide range of topical services published by Bureau of National

Affairs, which are also available by subscription on the Bloomberg BNA website. Some topical services are available from multiple online providers. For example, *The Standard Federal Tax Reporter* is available to subscribers on Lexis Advance and on Westlaw, as well as from its publisher on a research platform called CCH IntelliConnect.[21]

Most online topical services allow you to browse or use a full-text search. A challenge for some researchers using online topical services is to distinguish carefully between primary and secondary source material. Because primary and secondary source material may look similar in an online format, always be careful to confirm whether material you are looking at is primary or secondary authority.

V. *American Law Reports*

American Law Reports (ALR) publishes commentary on narrow issues of law.[22] These articles are called "annotations." Annotations provide a survey of the law in different jurisdictions on the topic of the annotation. The text of an annotation on the exact topic of your research may provide particularly useful background, and the citations may provide valuable entry points for research. Do not, however, cite an ALR annotation as persuasive authority. Although ALR annotations are written by knowledgeable lawyers, the authors of ALR annotations are generally not recognized experts whose views would persuade a court.

In print, ALR has been published in several series. The first through third series of ALR include annotations and cases on both state and federal law. Federal law topics are now included in ALR Fed., ALR Fed. 2d, and ALR Fed. 3d. State law topics are addressed in ALR 4th through ALR 7th.

Individual ALR annotations generally include an outline, an index, and a jurisdictional table to lead you to the precise information you are looking for within the annotation. Annotations are updated with pocket parts that provide citations to cases that were decided after the annotation was published.

---

21. The contractual arrangements by which the major vendors provide access to publications from other companies change over time; thus, it is advisable to check whether or not a particular title is available on a particular service.

22. ALR is published by West. It is available on both Lexis Advance and Westlaw. It is not currently available on Bloomberg Law.

To locate an ALR annotation in print, use the *ALR Index*, which covers all the print series of ALR. This index is in ten volumes, which are arranged alphabetically. To search this index, use the descriptive-word method, using one of the techniques for generating search terms discussed in Chapter 2. In addition to index entries, each volume of the *ALR Index* includes an annotation history table. When your index search leads you to a potentially relevant annotation, use this table to determine whether the annotation has been supplemented or superseded by a more recent annotation. The *ALR Index*, including its annotation history tables, is updated quarterly with pocket parts.

Alternatively, you may use the *ALR Quick Index*, which covers the third through sixth series of ALR, or the *ALR Federal Quick Index*, which covers both federal series. These indexes, which are updated periodically, are less comprehensive than the *ALR Index*.

To locate an ALR annotation on Lexis Advance or Westlaw, you can conduct a full-text search and filter your search to ALR, or you can browse to the source and search within it.

VI. Continuing Legal Education Materials

Unlike many jurisdictions, Massachusetts currently has no mandatory continuing legal education (CLE) requirement to maintain membership in the bar of the Commonwealth. Nonetheless, organizations such as Massachusetts Continuing Legal Education (MCLE) and the Massachusetts and Boston bar associations sponsor a wide range of continuing legal education programs for Massachusetts lawyers. A course may be led by a practitioner, a judge, or a law professor. Topics range from accounting and finance for lawyers to prosecuting and defending homicide cases to representing non-profits. Some courses are aimed at new lawyers just learning the fundamentals of practice; however, many courses offer insights on cutting-edge legal issues. Even though Massachusetts has no CLE requirement, these programs are generally well attended.

Materials prepared in connection with CLE courses are useful secondary sources because they may include concise explanations of the law, with citations to authority; sample documents; and sample forms. Thus, a lawyer who is unfamiliar with an area of law or type of transaction may find guidance that is unavailable elsewhere.

Massachusetts CLE materials are available in law libraries, on Lexis Advance, Westlaw, and Bloomberg Law, and from the sponsoring organization. For example, MCLE has an extensive catalog of materials that is available on its website and in some Massachusetts law libraries.[23] Many of the major titles are available on Lexis Advance, Westlaw, or Bloomberg Law. To search for CLE material in print, search the library catalog by topic or by author, using the names of the more common CLE publishers as search terms.

VII. Legal Encyclopedias

Like other encyclopedias, legal encyclopedias provide general information on a variety of subjects. Although encyclopedias offer a general sense about an area of law, their primary usefulness as secondary authority lies in their citations to primary authority, which provide entry points to research. Thus, an encyclopedia may help you get started on a research project even when the encyclopedia's text has not been recently updated.

The two national legal encyclopedias are *Corpus Juris Secundum* (CJS) and *American Jurisprudence, Second Edition* (Am Jur 2d). Figure 3-3 shows a short excerpt from Am Jur 2d.

In print, legal encyclopedias are organized by subject matter under "topics," which are presented alphabetically in bound volumes. To find relevant material, use the general index to the encyclopedia, ordinarily found at the end of the set, or pull the volume that contains the topic you are researching. The text of most encyclopedia entries is cursory because the goal of the writers is to summarize the law. Encyclopedia entries identify significant variations that exist between different jurisdictions, but they do not attempt to resolve differences or recommend improvements in the law. Pocket parts sometimes provide updated commentary.

The footnotes that accompany the text are the most helpful feature of an encyclopedia, especially if they refer to recent primary authority from your jurisdiction. However, because the footnotes in CJS and Am Jur 2d cite to authorities from all American jurisdictions and tend to be dated, the chance of finding a reference to a recent, relevant case is limited. The encyclopedia's pocket parts may offer better prospects for researching recent primary authority.

An encyclopedia may provide cross-references to other sources. For example, CJS includes cross-references to relevant topics and key numbers in West's digests, so a citation to even an older case may be a useful entry point. Similarly, Am Jur 2d cross-references ALR, discussed earlier in this chapter, a source of entry points.

---

23. Other publishers of CLE material include Practising Law Institute (PLI), the American Law Institute (ALI), and the American Bar Association (ABA).

Figure 3-3. Excerpt from "Contracts" in Am Jur 2d

§ 227   17A AM JUR 2d

even though it is in fact a new agreement.[5] Where the original promise is tainted with illegality, the taint cannot be removed by a new promise based on the old one.[6]

§ 228 Illegality in performance as affecting validity of contract

Research References

8 Williston on Contracts (4th ed.) § 19:40
West's Key Number Digest, Contracts ☞101(1), 103

An agreement which cannot be performed without a violation of the law is illegal and void,[1] whether or not the parties knew the law.[2] However, under some authority, where a contract could have been performed in a legal manner as well as in an illegal manner, it will not be declared void because it was in fact performed in an illegal manner,[3] at least if the performance is not seriously injurious to the public order.[4] Nor will a contract be declared void because it might have been performed in an illegal manner,[5] since bad motives are never to be imputed to any person where fair and honest intentions are sufficient to account for his or her conduct.[6]

On the other hand, there is authority that contracts based on a legitimate subject matter that are performed in an unlawful manner may be unenforceable.[7] There is also authority that while a lawful contract is not rendered illegal by illegal acts in performance, the right to recover under it may be defeated by an illegal performance.[8] It has also been held that an agreement entered into with an intent to violate the law is illegal even if the parties may, in performing it, depart from the agreement and keep within the law.[9]

---

[5]§ 304.

[6]Smilansky v. Mandel Bros., 254 Mich. 575, 236 N.W. 866 (1931).

[Section 228]

[1]Yankton Sioux Tribe of Indians v. U.S., 272 U.S. 351, 47 S. Ct. 142, 71 L. Ed. 294 (1926); Keith Furnace Co. v. Mac Vicar, 225 Iowa 246, 280 N.W. 496 (1938).

A contract to do a thing which cannot be done without a violation of the law is void. Lewis v. Davis, 145 Tex. 468, 199 S.W.2d 146 (1947).

[2]Miller v. Thompson, 40 Nev. 35, 160 P. 775 (1916); Texas Employers' Ins. Ass'n v. Tabor, 283 S.W. 779 (Tex. Comm'n App. 1926).

[3]Platt v. Wells Fargo Bank Am. Trust Co., 222 Cal. App. 2d 658, 35 Cal. Rptr. 377 (1st

Dist. 1963); Meissner v. Caravello, 4 Ill. App. 2d 428, 124 N.E.2d 615 (1st Dist. 1954); Keith Furnace Co. v. Mac Vicar, 225 Iowa 246, 280 N.W. 496 (1938).

[4]Meissner v. Caravello, 4 Ill. App. 2d 428, 124 N.E.2d 615 (1st Dist. 1954).

[5]Meissner v. Caravello, 4 Ill. App. 2d 428, 124 N.E.2d 615 (1st Dist. 1954).

[6]Meissner v. Caravello, 4 Ill. App. 2d 428, 124 N.E.2d 615 (1st Dist. 1954).

[7]U.S. Nursing Corp. v. Saint Joseph Medical Center, 39 F.3d 790 (7th Cir. 1994) (applying Illinois law).

[8]Tocci v. Lembo, 325 Mass. 707, 92 N.E.2d 254 (1950).

[9]Keith Furnace Co. v. Mac Vicar, 225 Iowa 246, 280 N.W. 496 (1938).

232

Source: 17A Am. Jur. 2d *Contracts* § 228, page 232 (2004). Reprinted with permission of Thomson Reuters.

Am Jur 2d and CJS are published by West and are available in print and on-line. Both are available on Westlaw, but only Am Jur 2d is available on Lexis Advance. Bloomberg Law currently does not include these encyclopedias.

VIII. Restatements of the Law, Uniform Laws, and Model Acts

Restatements, uniform laws, and model acts are different from most other secondary sources because, instead of presenting narrative explanation of an area of law, these publications propose rules of law and provide commentary on those proposed rules. When rules in these publications are adopted by a jurisdiction, they become primary authority within the jurisdiction. These publications are drafted by committees of judges, scholars, legislators, and practitioners. Thus, even when the commentary of the drafters is not explicitly adopted along with the rules, commentary may be very persuasive because it presents views of highly regarded bodies on how the law should develop in a given area and the reasoning underlying those views.

A. Restatements

The *Restatements of the Law* are publications of the American Law Institute (ALI), a highly regarded body of legal scholars, judges, and lawyers, which was founded in 1923. Restatements are intended to clarify and synthesize principles of law in a given area.[24] The initial draft of a restatement is prepared by a reporter, an expert in the area covered by the restatement, who is appointed by the ALI to head the given project. In addition to articulating principles of law, restatements provide accompanying interpretive material in the form of comments, illustrations, and reporter's notes. Restatements are useful research tools because they present detailed and organized analysis of the law and cite the primary authority on which the analysis is based. Thus, restatements are useful both as aids to understanding the law and as finding tools.

When a court decides to adopt a restatement's articulation of a principle of law, the court will cite the restatement as authority and may also refer to the restatement's comments on the principle.[25] When the court refers to this material explicitly, it becomes part of the law of the jurisdiction. Even when the court adopting a restatement rule does not explicitly refer to the restatement's interpretive material, that material is likely to be persuasive to a later court.

Restatements are issued in series. The first series of the *Restatements*, issued between 1923 and 1944, included restatements of the law of agency, contracts,

---

24. For a list of restatements, see the website of the American Law Institute at www.ali.org.
25. *See Rae v. Air-Speed, Inc.*, 386 Mass. 187, 194 (1982).

conflict of laws, judgments, property, security, restitution, and torts. Most of these restatements were revised and reissued in the second series.[26] Current restatements are in the third series, whether or not there was an earlier version. For example, the *Restatement (Third) of Unfair Competition* is the first version of that restatement. Remember: restatements are secondary, not primary, authority. Thus, if a jurisdiction has adopted a principle of law from the first series of a restatement, and the ALI issues a second or third series that changes the principle, the law remains as stated in the first series unless and until the jurisdiction adopts the change.

Restatements are accessible in print and on Lexis Advance, Westlaw, and HeinOnline.[27] Pocket parts to the print restatements update the annotations to authority in the print volumes. Updated annotations are also available on Lexis Advance and Westlaw. Before searching for restatement rules or annotations on Lexis Advance or Westlaw, consult the information icon for source. This review will help you confirm that this source is appropriate for your search and also provide you with tips for constructing your search.

B. Uniform Laws

Uniform Laws are drafted by the National Conference of Commissioners on Uniform State Laws (NCCUSL), also known as the Uniform Law Commission, which was established in 1892 to draft legislation that is consistent from state to state. Uniform laws have no effect unless they are adopted by a state legislature. Widely adopted uniform laws include the Uniform Commercial Code, which has been adopted by every state; the Uniform Partnership Act; and the Uniform Electronic Transfers Act. Uniform laws adopted by at least one jurisdiction are included in *Uniform Laws Annotated*,[28] which includes the text of uniform laws, the commissioners' notes on each law, and annotations to cases from adopting jurisdictions. This title also includes commentaries and notes regarding differences in various enacted state laws.

Uniform Laws Annotated is available in a multi-volume print set, which is updated regularly. To get access to the *Uniform Laws Annotated* database on Westlaw, browse to Statutes and Court Rules, and then select *Uniform Laws Annotated* from the "Tools and Resources" list. Individual uniform acts are

---

26. An example of a restatement in the second series is the *Restatement (Second) of Conflict of Laws*.

27. Restatements are not accessible in full text from the website of the American Law Institute.

28. *Uniform Laws Annotated* is published by West.

available on Lexis Advance, Bloomberg Law, and HeinOnline. The text of uniform acts and other information, including archives, are available at the organization's website.[29]

C. Model Acts

Model acts are drafted by the Uniform Law Commission or by ALI. Examples of adopted model acts are the Model Business Corporations Act and the Model Survival and Death Act. There is no centralized collection of all model acts. Some are available in print sets or as sources on Lexis Advance, Westlaw, Bloomberg Law, or HeinOnline.

IX. Forms and Jury Instructions

A. Forms

Some statutes prescribe forms or precise language that a document must include. In other situations, a form can be a great shortcut in drafting a legal document, especially a document you are drafting for the first time in an unfamiliar area of law.

Large legal employers maintain electronic databases of forms used in their practice. If you do not have access to this type of database, *Mass. Practice* is a good first stop in a search for forms. Many other practitioner-oriented publications, especially CLE publications, in print or online, include forms. Bloomberg Law has a vast collection of forms. Lexis Advance and Westlaw include general form databases, which can be located by browsing or full-text searching.

Use forms carefully. Before using a form, you may need to do legal research to make sure that the form accurately reflects the relevant law of your jurisdiction.

B. Jury Instructions

Published sets of jury instructions outline the law; in other words, they tell a lawyer preparing for trial what she has to prove in order to prevail. Examining these instructions in advance of trial may influence an attorney's decisions on how to present evidence during trial. Because jury instructions identify legal

---

29. The URL is www.uniformlaws.org.

requirements, they may be helpful research resources even in matters that are not litigated.

Counsel almost uniformly give the judge requested jury instructions, so it is important to know how to find models for appropriate instructions. You can locate collections of form jury instructions reflecting Massachusetts law in print in most law libraries, in MCLE publications, and on Lexis Advance and Westlaw. For civil cases, no pattern jury instructions are approved by Massachusetts courts, but the courts have issued model jury instructions for some criminal cases. In March 2013, the Supreme Judicial Court released new model jury instructions for homicide cases.[30] These are not required, but they should be used unless in a given case the judge finds that a different instruction would more accurately or clearly state the law. The District Court Department of the Trial Court issues *Model Criminal Jury Instructions for Use in the District Court,* which it updates and revises from time to time.[31]

---

30. This document is available in full text at http://www.mass.gov/courts/court-info/sjc/attorneys-bar-applicants/model-jury-inst-homicide-gen.html. The text of the instructions can also be found in print in law libraries and in MCLE materials on Lexis Advance and Westlaw.

31. This document is available in full text on the Massachusetts court website, mass.gov, under tabs for Court Information and Trial Court. The specific address is http://www.mass.gov/courts/court-info/trial-court/dc/dc-crim-model-jury-inst-gen .html. The instructions are also available in MCLE materials on Lexis Advance and Westlaw.

Chapter 4

Judicial Opinions

I. Introduction

Judicial opinions, which lawyers generally refer to as "cases," are issued by courts to explain their decisions in the matters they decide. As an official statement of a government unit, a judicial opinion is primary legal authority. Historically, only appellate courts issued opinions because only decisions of appellate courts in a given court system are mandatory authority for lower courts within that court system.[1] But even though a ruling of a trial court is not *formally* binding on another court, an opinion of a trial court may be persuasive authority.[2] In part for that reason, trial courts, especially in the federal system, increasingly publish opinions explaining their decisions.

Knowing which court issued a case is essential to legal problem solving because that determines the authority of the case with respect to a given problem. Thus, this chapter begins with an overview of the Massachusetts and federal court systems.[3] Then it goes on to discuss sources for Massachusetts judicial opinions. Chapter 5 discusses ways you can use print and online resources to find potentially relevant cases, sort cases for relevance, and then expand and validate your case law research.

II. Court Systems

The Massachusetts court system follows the basic structure of court systems throughout the United States, which includes a trial court, an intermediate

---

1. Chapter 1 discusses case law as legal authority.
2. Chapter 1 discusses the distinction between mandatory and persuasive authority.
3. The official website of the Massachusetts court system is www.mass.gov/courts. The official website for the federal judiciary is www.uscourts.gov.

court of appeals, and a court of appeals of last resort, often called the "supreme" court.[4] This three-level court hierarchy characterizes both state and federal court systems.[5]

A. Massachusetts Courts

The highest court in Massachusetts is the Supreme Judicial Court, generally referred to as the SJC. Beneath the SJC in the court hierarchy is the Appeals Court of Massachusetts, and beneath the Appeals Court is the Massachusetts Trial Court.[6] Figure 4-1 is a detailed chart of the Massachusetts court system.

Figure 4-1. The Massachusetts Court System

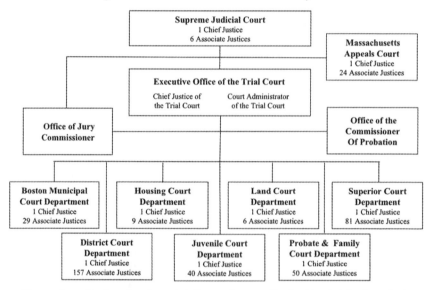

The number of justices for all courts is the maximum authorized by statute; the actual number of judges varies depending on vacancies.

Source: http://www.mass.gov/courts/docs/sjc/docs/court-sys-chart-2012.pdf.

---

4. The "supreme court" of a state is not always its highest court. In New York, for example, the Supreme Court is the trial court of general jurisdiction; the intermediate appellate court is the Supreme Court, Appellate Division; and the highest court is the Court of Appeals.

5. In the federal court system, the highest court is the United States Supreme Court. Beneath the Supreme Court are the thirteen United States Courts of Appeals, and the federal trial courts, including the United States District Courts and specialized trial courts.

6. The current court structure is the result of comprehensive statutory court reorganization in 1978. *See* 1978 Mass. Acts ch. 478. Before this court reform, Massachusetts

1. Massachusetts Trial Court

The Massachusetts Trial Court is a single court with seven departments.[7] It has two tiers of general jurisdiction: the Superior Court Department and the District Court Department. Although the Boston Municipal Court Department is similar to the District Court Department, it is a separate department serving the City of Boston. The Trial Court also has four specialized courts: the Juvenile Court Department, the Housing Court Department, the Land Court Department, and the Probate and Family Court Department.

The Superior Court generally handles the weightiest matters. It has exclusive, original jurisdiction in first-degree murder cases and has exclusive authority to convene medical malpractice tribunals. Its original jurisdiction includes civil actions in which the likely recovery exceeds $25,000, matters in which equitable relief is sought, and all crimes. The Superior Court shares jurisdiction over crimes where other Trial Court Departments have concurrent jurisdiction. It has an appellate division that hears appeals from certain sentences of imprisonment. It also hears appeals from certain administrative decisions.

The divisions of the District Court Department are geographically based, for example, the Hingham Division and the Springfield Division. The District Court's jurisdiction includes civil cases in which the likely recovery does not exceed $25,000, felonies punishable by a sentence of up to five years, some felonies with greater penalties, and all misdemeanors. The Appellate Division of the District Court sits in three-judge panels to review questions of law that arise in civil cases.

The geographical jurisdiction of the Boston Municipal Court covers certain parts of Boston. Its subject matter jurisdiction includes a wide variety of civil matters and criminal offenses that do not require a state prison sentence. It also has an appellate division.

The remaining departments of the Trial Court have specialized subject matter jurisdiction. In some situations, the jurisdiction of a specialized court is concurrent with the jurisdiction of the Superior Court, the District Court, or the Boston Municipal Court.

---

had no intermediate appellate court. In addition to creating the Appeals Court and making other changes, the court reorganization of 1978 organized the various trial courts of the Commonwealth into a single Trial Court with seven departments.

7. See www.mass.gov/courts/ for links to detailed descriptions of the Departments of the Massachusetts Trial Court.

2. Massachusetts Appellate Courts

As a general rule, appeals from the various Trial Court departments, including from appellate divisions, go in the first instance to the Appeals Court of Massachusetts. Notable exceptions are appeals from convictions for first-degree murder, which go directly to the SJC. The Appeals Court also has jurisdiction over appeals from certain administrative agencies.[8]

The SJC has very broad appellate jurisdiction.[9] With few exceptions, however, appeals must first be filed in the Appeals Court.[10] The SJC may grant direct appellate review before a decision of the Appeals Court, or may grant further appellate review after a decision of the Appeals Court. Except for cases designated by statute to be heard by the SJC, the SJC's review is discretionary.

In addition to its function as the appeals court of last resort in the Commonwealth, the SJC has several other functions. It is responsible for the general superintendence of the courts and of the bar of the Commonwealth, and it renders advisory opinions to the Governor and to the state legislature, most frequently on the constitutionality of proposed legislation.[11] The Associate Justices of the SJC sit weekly, on a rotating basis, as Single Justices to hear a variety of matters, including interlocutory appeals in criminal cases and bar discipline proceedings.[12]

B. Federal Courts

In the federal judicial system, the trial courts of general jurisdiction are called United States District Courts. Specialized trial-level courts include the Court of Federal Claims and International Trade Court.

There are ninety-four district courts in the federal system, with each district drawn from a single state. Some states are subdivided into several federal districts, but a state with a relatively small population or geographic area might not be subdivided. The entire Commonwealth of Massachusetts, for example,

---

8. See www.mass.gov/courts/ for a link to a more detailed description of the Appeals Court.

9. See www.mass.gov/courts/court-info/sjc for a link to a more detailed description of the SJC.

10. For example, as noted above, an appeal for a conviction of first-degree murder is filed directly in the SJC. Mass. Gen. Laws ch. 278, § 33E.

11. *See* Mass. Const. pt. 2, ch. 3, art. 2.

12. See http://www.mass.gov/courts/court-info/appealscourt/appeals-court-help-center/appeals-court-single-justice-practice.html for a detailed description of Single Justice practice.

makes up the District of Massachusetts.[13] Even though Massachusetts has a single federal judicial district, the district court sits in three cities: Boston, Springfield, and Worcester.

States with larger populations and higher caseloads have more districts. For example, New York has four federal districts: Northern, Southern, Eastern, and Western. California also has four federal districts: Northern, Central, Southern, and Eastern. Each federal district includes a Bankruptcy Court.

Intermediate appellate courts in the federal system are called United States Courts of Appeals. There is a court of appeals for each of the thirteen federal circuits.[14] Twelve of these circuits are determined by geography. Eleven numbered circuits cover all the states and territories; the twelfth is the District of Columbia Circuit. The thirteenth federal circuit, called the Federal Circuit, hears appeals from district courts in all other circuits on issues related to patent law and from certain specialized courts and agencies. Cases from the United States District Court for the District of Massachusetts are appealed to the United States Court of Appeals for the First Circuit, along with cases from Maine, New Hampshire, Rhode Island, and Puerto Rico.[15]

The highest court in the federal system is the United States Supreme Court. It decides cases arising under the United States Constitution and federal statutes. The Court does not have the final say on matters of purely state law; that authority rests with the highest court of each state. Although in limited circumstances parties may appeal as of right to the U.S. Supreme Court, ordinarily a party must file a petition for *certiorari*, as the Court has discretion over whether or not to hear most cases.

III. Case Reporting

A. In Print

Before the advent of electronic media, judicial opinions were maintained only in print volumes called "reporters."[16] A print reporter publishes decisions

---

13. The official website of the District of Massachusetts is www.mad.uscourts.gov.

14. These are called "circuits" because originally, the Supreme Court Justices "rode circuit" to sit with federal district judges on courts in each federal judicial district.

15. The official website of the First Circuit is www.ca1.uscourts.gov.

16. Official case reporting goes back to at least sixteenth century England. *See* J.H. Baker, *An Introduction to English Legal History* 179 (2002). Today, a case is first published in print as a "slip opinion," a report of a single case released by a court. Publishers of print reporters collect cases in soft-cover pamphlets called "advance sheets" that are is-

of a single court or a group of courts, following roughly chronological order. While researchers increasingly use electronic resources, print reporters remain in wide use. But even researchers who work primarily with electronic resources must be familiar with how cases are reported in print because the generally accepted system of legal citation—which provides the "address" of a case— is based on the organization of print reporters by volume and page.[17]

1. Print Reporters

There are two main classifications of print reporters: official and unofficial. Official reporters are published by or under the auspices of a governmental unit. Unofficial reporters are published commercially. Today, West is the main commercial reporter of decisions of federal[18] and state courts; it also publishes the official reports of some states.

The courts of some states—the SJC and Appeals Court of Massachusetts included—require citation to the official reporter. For purposes of ordinary legal research, however, there is no other reason to prefer the official *Massachusetts Reports* over the unofficial *North Eastern Reporter*, published by West.

Decisions of the SJC are published officially in the *Massachusetts Reports*.[19] The case *Austin v. Austin*, 445 Mass. 601 (2005), appears in volume 445 of the

---

sued at short intervals. The opinions in several issues of advance sheets are compiled in bound volumes of the print reporter, where they are maintained permanently.

17. *See generally* ALWD & Colleen M. Barger, *ALWD Guide to Citation* (5th ed., Wolters Kluwer Law & Business 2014) (*ALWD Guide*) and *The Bluebook: A Uniform System of Citation* (The Columbia Law Review et al. eds., 20th ed. 2015) (*The Bluebook*). The Association of American Law Libraries has advocated a "universal" system of citation that is not based on physical characteristics of books. *See Report of the AALL Task Force on Citation Formats*, 87 L. Libr. J. 577 (1995). The SJC Reporter of Decisions has issued a *Style Manual* used by the Justices, their law clerks, and the staffs of the office of the Reporter of Decisions, and "may be useful to those preparing appellate briefs." The *Style Manual* advises that *it* is now the "guidepost" and that *The Bluebook*, which was previously followed, should be consulted only when the *Style Manual* refers to it or when the *Style Manual* is silent on a particular matter. The *Style Manual* may be found on the website of the Reporter of Decisions at http://www.mass.gov/courts/docs/sjc/docs/reporter-of-decisions-style-guide.pdf.

18. For decisions of the United States Supreme Court, there is the official *United States Reports*. West publishes the unofficial *Supreme Court Reports* and LexisNexis publishes the unofficial *United States Supreme Court Reports, Lawyers' Edition*, now in its second series. There is no official reporter of the decisions of the lower federal courts. Thus, for decisions from these courts, researchers use West reporters.

19. *Massachusetts Reports* publishes all SJC opinions, advisory opinions of the SJC, the text of rules promulgated directly by the SJC, and the SJC's disposition of applica-

Massachusetts Reports beginning at page 601.[20] Decisions of the Appeals Court are published officially in the *Massachusetts Appeals Court Reports*. The case *Colorio v. Marx*, 72 Mass. App. Ct. 382 (2008), is found in volume 72 of the *Massachusetts Appeals Court Reports*, starting on page 382.

Decisions of the SJC and the Appeals Court are issued first as slip opinions, without final citation information.[21] They are also published officially in weekly online advance sheets, which have final volume and page designations.[22] *Massachusetts Lawyers Weekly*, the leading commercial legal newspaper, publishes summaries of cases in print shortly after they are decided and provides access on its website to recent opinions of Massachusetts appellate and other courts.[23] The decisions of the Appellate Divisions of the District Court and the Boston Municipal Court Departments have been reported since 1980 in the *Massachusetts Appellate Division Reports* and before 1980 in a variety of reporters and advance sheets.[24]

Decisions of both the SJC and the Appeals Court are published unofficially in West's *North Eastern Reporter*. This is a *regional reporter* that also includes decisions from courts in Illinois, Indiana, New York, and Ohio. Cases in the *North Eastern Reporter* and in West's other regional reporters are first issued in weekly advance sheets, which are later compiled into bound volumes. West

---

tions for further appellate review of a decision of the Appeals Court. In 2014, LexisNexis became the publisher of the official *Massachusetts Reports* and *Massachusetts Appeals Court Reports*.

20. Between 1822 and 1867 the volumes of the official reports of decisions of the SJC were designated with the name of the reporter of decisions instead of being numbered as volumes of the *Massachusetts Reports*. Thus, *Commonwealth v. Hackett*, 2 Allen 136 (1861), would be found in volume 2 of the *Allen Reporter*. These volumes have been incorporated into the *Massachusetts Reports* as volumes 17 through 97, but for these volumes, the citation must refer to the name of the reporter of decisions instead of to the volume number. Mass. R. App. P. 16(g); *see Style Manual* at 4. Thus, a lawyer submitting a brief to a Massachusetts appellate court would use the *Allen*, and not the *Massachusetts Reports*, volume designation.

21. Slip opinions of SJC and Appeals Court decisions are available at http://www.mass.gov/courts/court-info/sjc/about/reporter-of-decisions/new-opinions.html. You may register at the website to receive e-mail notification of new slip opinions.

22. Official Massachusetts Advance Sheets are available in e-book form by paid subscription through LexisNexis.

23. The website is www.masslawyersweekly.com.

24. These decisions are binding only on the trial divisions of the District Court and Boston Municipal Court. For a complete list of dates and publications, see *The Bluebook* at 270.

also publishes a separate series called *Massachusetts Decisions*, which contains only the Massachusetts decisions published in the *North Eastern Reporter*.

The *North Eastern Reporter* is part of West's National Reporter System, which divides the 50 states and the District of Columbia into seven regions: Atlantic, North Eastern, North Western, Pacific, South Eastern, South Western, and Southern.[25] Table 4-1 shows West's groupings of states into its regions.

Table 4-1. Regional Reporters and States Included

Atlantic Reporter (A., A.2d, A.3d)	Connecticut, Delaware, District of Columbia, Maine, Maryland, New Hampshire, New Jersey, Pennsylvania, Rhode Island, and Vermont
North Eastern Reporter (N.E., N.E.2d, N.E.3d)	Illinois, Indiana, Massachusetts, New York, and Ohio
North Western Reporter (N.W., N.W.2d)	Iowa, Michigan, Minnesota, Nebraska, North Dakota, South Dakota, and Wisconsin
Pacific Reporter (P., P.2d, P.3d)	Alaska, Arizona, California, Colorado, Hawaii, Idaho, Kansas, Montana, Nevada, New Mexico, Oklahoma, Oregon, Utah, Washington, and Wyoming
South Eastern Reporter (S.E., S.E.2d)	Georgia, North Carolina, South Carolina, Virginia, and West Virginia
South Western Reporter (S.W., S.W.2d, S.W.3d)	Arkansas, Kentucky, Missouri, Tennessee, and Texas
Southern Reporter (So., So. 2d, So. 3d)	Alabama, Florida, Louisiana, and Mississippi

In legal publishing, when a reporter reaches a certain volume number, the publisher begins another "series." The first series of the *North Eastern Reporter* closed with volume 200 in 1936, and the second series closed with volume 999 in 2014. The reporter is now in its third series. When a reporter has multiple series, the series designation of the volume is a crucial part of the citation of a case.

---

25. West grouped the states into its regions in the late nineteenth century, and thus, some of the groupings (for example, placing Kansas cases in the *Pacific Reporter*) do not make sense today. Moreover, the West regions do not correspond to the federal judicial circuits.

The West print reporters include editorial enhancements that can make research more efficient. These enhancements connect different print sources published by West in addition to connecting West's print sources with electronic resources on Westlaw. West's print reports of cases and the versions of cases on Lexis Advance, Westlaw, and Bloomberg Law include features that allow the researcher to cite to a page in the official reporter even when using an unofficial version of the case. If the official citation of a case is available when West prints the unofficial version of the case, West includes the official citation above the title of the case. This citation shows the volume and first page of the case in the official reporter. Within the case, West uses a symbol to indicate the specific page on which text in the West print report of the case occurs in the official reporter. Figure 4-2 shows an excerpt of a West print report of a case with the symbol indicating the page on which the text occurs in the official reporter. In this excerpt, the symbol with the number 815 together indicate that the text that follows is on page 815 of the official reporter volume.

Figure 4-2. West Print Version of Case Showing Corresponding Page Number in Official Reporter

> COWIN, J.
>
> The plaintiffs, former clients of the defendant, an attorney, brought suit against him alleging negligence, breach of $|_{815}$contract, and violations of G.L. c. 93A, § 11, arising from his representation of them during the course of earlier litigation. In allowing the defendant's motion for summary judgment, a judge of the Superior Court determined that evidence that the defendant's negligence caused loss to the plaintiffs was insufficient to warrant a finding in their favor. He concluded also

Source: *North Eastern Reporter.* Reprinted with permission of Thomson Reuters.

Lexis Advance, Westlaw, and Bloomberg Law allow you to see the pagination of cases in the applicable official and print reporters as well as each service's own pagination. Consult each service for its specific pagination system.

Not all cases are "published." For example, the Appeals Court decides many cases by summary order under Appeals Court Rule 1:28. Under longstanding practice of the court, these decisions could not be cited. In 2008, however, the Appeals Court announced that it was changing this practice,[26] and a rule change to confirm that these unpublished decisions could be cited took effect January 1, 2009. Currently, summary dispositions of the Appeals Court issued on or after February 25, 2008, may be cited for persuasive value, but not as binding precedent. Other than the prior practice under Rule 1:28, Massachusetts courts do not formally prohibit citing unpublished or otherwise non-precedential decisions, which apparently may be cited for their persuasive value.[27]

2. Features of Cases in Print Reporters

In print reporters, a case includes the full text of the court's decision, as well as other material added either by the court's staff or by the editors of the commercial publisher. This material includes the parties to the case, its docket number, the name of the court issuing the opinion, the date of the decision, the name of the judge who wrote the opinion for the court, and the names of the other judges who participated in the decision. If the court did not decide the case unanimously, the report of the decision will include concurring or dissenting opinions.

In addition to this material, most cases in print reporters include summaries of the points of law in the opinions. For Massachusetts cases, these summaries are prepared by the Reporter of Decisions, who is charged by statute with preparing opinions for publication in the official reporters.[28] Editors at West prepare summaries for cases published in the *North Eastern Reporter*.[29] The number and content of headnotes for the same case will differ in the official and unofficial reporters. Figure 4-3 shows the first page of *Bortolotti v. Hayden*,

---

26. *See Chace v. Curran*, 71 Mass. App. Ct. 258, 260–61 n. 4 (2008).

27. Although a lawyer may never *rely* on the reasoning of an unpublished decision of an appellate court or an otherwise non-precedential decision, these decisions may include careful reasoning that may be persuasive. Unpublished opinions are increasingly available electronically, so researchers encounter them often. Rule 32.1 of the Federal Rules of Appellate Procedure makes clear that unpublished opinions may be cited, although local rules may restrict their precedential value.

28. The website of the Massachusetts Reporter of Decisions is http://www.mass.gov/courts/court-info/sjc/about/reporter-of-decisions/.

29. The West summaries, in the form of numbered headnotes, are the foundation of a powerful research tool called the West Key Number System. Chapter 5 discusses this tool.

449 Mass. 193 (2007), as it appears in the *Massachusetts Reports*. Figure 4-4 shows the first two pages of *Bortolotti* as it appears in the *North Eastern Reporter*. Figure 4-5 shows an excerpt from *Bortolotti* as it appears on Westlaw.

B. In Online Sources

Massachusetts cases are available through many online sources. Many of these sources require a subscription, although cases are increasingly available through free internet resources.

The website of the Reporter of Decisions offers free access to slip opinions, electronic versions of the official reports of the SJC and the Appeals Court, and unpublished decisions of the Appeals Court in separate searchable databases.

Commercial research services offer their subscribers extensive coverage of Massachusetts cases. Lexis Advance, Westlaw, and Bloomberg Law have full coverage of SJC and Appeals Court cases. They also have decisions of the Superior Court and the appellate divisions of the District Court and the Boston Municipal Court. Extensive Massachusetts case coverage is also available from other services, such as Fastcase, Ravel Law, and VersusLaw. The editorial features of opinions vary from service to service, as do the costs of use. Members of the Massachusetts Bar Association have access to Casemaker, which has libraries of federal and Massachusetts primary authorities, including cases.

Massachusetts decisions are also available through free internet resources. SJC and Appeals Court decisions are available on Google Scholar. In addition, the Massachusetts Trial Court Law Libraries maintain masscases.com, which contains cases from the SJC, Appeals Court, Land Court, and Appellate Division of the District Court.

Figure 4-3. First Page of *Bortolotti v. Hayden* in *Massachusetts Reports*

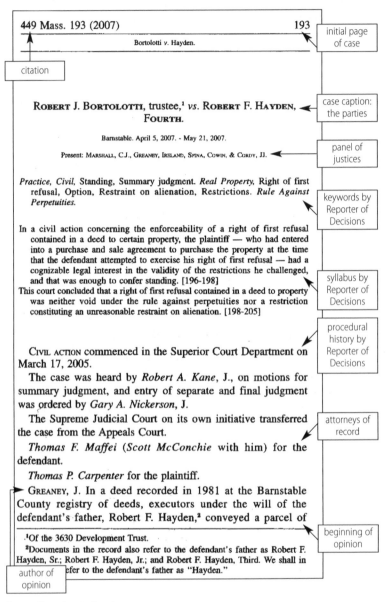

Figure 4-4. Opening Two Pages of *Bortolotti v. Hayden* in *North Eastern Reporter, Second Series*

West reporter volume

unofficial reporter citation:
882 N.E.2d 882 (Mass. 2007)

882 Mass.   866 NORTH EASTERN REPORTER, 2d SERIES

449 Mass. 193 ◄— official reporter citation

case caption: the parties

Robert J. BORTOLOTTI, trustee,[1]

v.

Robert F. HAYDEN, Fourth.

Supreme Judicial Court of Massachusetts, Barnstable.

date argued & date decided

Argued April 5, 2007.

Decided May 21, 2007.

Background: Failed purchaser brought action against grantor's son, seeking declaratory judgment that right of first refusal in deed violated rule against perpetuities and therefore was void and unenforceable. On motions for summary judgment, the Superior Court, Barnstable County, Robert A. Kane, J., entered judgment for failed purchaser. Grantor's son appealed, and the Supreme Judicial Court transferred the appeal on its own motion.

Holdings: The Supreme Judicial Court, Greaney, J., held that:

(1) failed purchaser had standing to bring action;

(2) as a matter of first impression, rule against perpetuities did not bar right of first refusal; and

(3) rule against restraints on alienation did not bar right of first refusal.

Reversed and remanded.

syllabus by West editor

1. Declaratory Judgment ⬥300

Failed purchaser had standing, in de-

...d purchaser had en-...se and sale agreement to purchase the property at the time that grantor's son attempted to exercise the right of first refusal, and that agreement did not state it would become null and void if right of first refusal was exercised. M.G.L.A. c. 231A, § 9.

headnote by West editor

2. Perpetuities ⬥4(1)

Common law rule against perpetuities did not bar right of first refusal contained in deed, which gave grantor's heirs and assigns the right to purchase the subject property on the same terms as any bona fide offer that grantee w[o]... which did not contain any ... tion.

West topic and key number

3. Appeal and Error ⬥863

The Supreme Judicial Court reviews an entry of summary judgment to determine whether the successful party has demonstrated that there is no genuine issue as to any material fact and that it is entitled to a judgment as matter of law.

4. Perpetuities ⬥4(1)

The rule against perpetuities is a doctrine that places a strict limit on how long certain types of property interests may continue.

5. Perpetuities ⬥4(1)

The common-law "rule against perpetuities" is traditionally defined as a rule

Source: *North Eastern Reporter.* Reprinted with permission of Thomson Reuters.

**Figure 4-4. Opening Two Pages of *Bortolotti v. Hayden* in
North Eastern Reporter, Second Series, continued**

BORTOLOTTI v. HAYDEN   Mass. **883**
Cite as 866 N.E.2d 882 (Mass. 2007)

6. Perpetuities ⚷4(1)

An option to purchase real estate at a fixed price falls within the common-law rule against perpetuities.

7. Vendor and Purchaser ⚷57

A true right of first refusal becomes operational when the owner has decided to accept a third person's outstanding and enforceable offer and the holder of the right has been informed of the details of that offer and has had a reasonable time to meet it.

8. Vendor and Purchaser ⚷57

A property owner's obligation under a right of first refusal is not to sell at such a time that the holder of the right may demand, as in option to purchase, or to sell to the holder at a fixed price at such a time as the owner should wish to sell, as in a fixed price right of first refusal, but merely to provide the holder of the right seasonable disclosure of the terms of any bona fide

[text at page 194 of volume 449 of the official *Massachusetts Reports*]

...table to the ... both to the ... may decide ...holder of the right, who may decide whether to purchase at the price offered by the third party.

9. Vendor and Purchaser ⚷57

At the time of a third-party offer that the owner has decided to accept, a right of first refusal ripens into an option to purchase according to the terms of the third-party offer.

11. Perpetuities ⚷6(1)

Rule against restraints on alienation did not bar right of first refusal contained in deed, which gave grantor's heirs and assigns the right to purchase the property on the same terms as any bona fide offer that grantee would accept and which did not contain any temporal limitation.

[additional West headnotes]   [attorneys of record]

Thomas F. Maffei, Boston (Scott McConchie with him) for the defendant.

Thomas P. Carpenter, Yarmouth, for the plaintiff.

[panel of justices]

Present: MARSHALL, C.J., GREANEY, IRELAND, SPINA, COWIN, & CORDY, JJ.

[author of opinion]

GREANEY, J.

┕₁₉₃In a deed recorded in 1981 at the Barnstable County registry of deeds, executors under the will of the defendant's father, Robert F. Hayden,[2] conveyed a parcel of ┕₁₉₄subdivided land situated "in Barnstable (Cotuit)" to Albert Mattson. A restriction in the deed reserved to the grantor's heirs, executors, administrators, and assigns, a preemptive right to purchase the property on the same terms and conditions contained in any bona fide offer received by, and acceptable to, the grantee, his heirs, executors, administrators, and assigns. The restrictive covenant, which we shall refer to as the right of first refusal, was not limited to a term of years,

Figure 4-5. Excerpt of *Bortolotti v. Hayden* on Westlaw

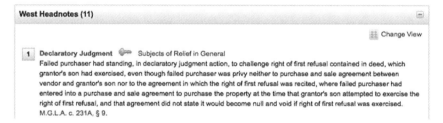

Original Image of 866 N.E.2d 882 (PDF)

449 Mass. 193
Supreme Judicial Court of Massachusetts,
Barnstable.

Robert J. BORTOLOTTI, trustee,[1]

v.

Robert F. HAYDEN, Fourth.

Argued April 5, 2007.
Decided May 21, 2007.

Synopsis
Background: Failed purchaser brought action against grantor's son, seeking declaratory judgment that right of first refusal in deed violated rule against perpetuities and therefore was void and unenforceable. On motions for summary judgment, the Superior Court, Barnstable County, Robert A. Kane, J., entered judgment for failed purchaser. Grantor's son appealed, and the Supreme Judicial Court transferred the appeal on its own motion.

Holdings: The Supreme Judicial Court, Greaney, J., held that:
1 failed purchaser had standing to bring action;
2 as a matter of first impression, rule against perpetuities did not bar right of first refusal; and
3 rule against restraints on alienation did not bar right of first refusal.

Reversed and remanded.

West Headnotes (11)

Change View

1 **Declaratory Judgment**   Subjects of Relief in General
Failed purchaser had standing, in declaratory judgment action, to challenge right of first refusal contained in deed, which grantor's son had exercised, even though failed purchaser was privy neither to purchase and sale agreement between vendor and grantor's son nor to the agreement in which the right of first refusal was recited, where failed purchaser had entered into a purchase and sale agreement to purchase the property at the time that grantor's son attempted to exercise the right of first refusal, and that agreement did not state it would become null and void if right of first refusal was exercised.
M.G.L.A. c. 231A, § 9.

Source: Westlaw. Used with permission of Thomson Reuters.

Chapter 5

Case Law Research

I. Introduction

A case is easy to find if you have its citation, just as you can generally find a building if you have its address and a good map. To find in print the *Bortolotti* case excerpted in Chapter 4, you would go to a law library and pull from the shelf either volume 449 of the *Massachusetts Reports* or volume 866 of the *North Eastern Reporter, Second Series*. On Lexis Advance, Westlaw, Bloomberg Law, and other commercial services, it is easy to type the citation into a search box and retrieve the case.

But most of the time you will not come armed with the citation to the case or cases you need — or even know which cases you are looking for. In this situation you will need to use research tools to identify the citations to the cases that you need to find. In the parlance of Chapter 2, you need an entry point. Table 5-1 gives an overview of pathways for case law research, beginning with different entry points for assembling a list of citations to potentially relevant cases.

II. Assembling a List of Potentially Relevant Cases

A. Using a Secondary Source or Annotations to a Statute

In many research projects where case law applies, your entry point into the group of relevant cases will be a secondary source or annotations to an applicable statute.[1] These sources will direct you to relevant cases, which in turn will cite other relevant cases, which you will then analyze as a group to gain

---

1. Chapter 2, § III.B.1, discusses using secondary sources and annotated codes as entry points.

Table 5-1. Steps for Case Law Research

Step #1	Use one or more of the following entry points to assemble a list of citations to *potentially* relevant cases: • a secondary source, • an annotated code, • subject searching in print or online, or • full-text searching online.
Step #2	Pare down your list of *potentially* relevant cases to a list of *probably* relevant cases: • skim or read headnotes of cases located through a secondary source, • read summaries of cases located through an annotated code, • read headnotes of cases located through subject searching, or • skim or read summaries or headnotes of cases found through a full-text search.
Step #3	Expand your list of cases by using different methods: • read cases cited by a leading case, • use a citator, • use subject searching in print or online, or • use a full-text search online.
Step #4	Carefully analyze the cases on your list to understand the applicable law. Be on the lookout for additional ideas to pursue.
Step #5	If you determine that additional research is needed, go back through Steps #1 through #4.
Step #6	If you haven't done so at an earlier step in this process, use a citator to validate every case on your list.

an understanding of the law that applies to your client's problem. The cases you find in this manner give you access to the West Key Number System, discussed below, through which you may find further relevant cases. Many projects will include full-text searching in a commercial research service. In every project you will use a citator,[2] such as online *Shepard's*,[3] KeyCite,[4] or BCite,[5] which allow you to both validate and expand your research.

---

2. Chapter 2 introduces citators.
3. *Shepard's* is available in print, but much easier to use on Lexis Advance.
4. KeyCite, West's citator, is available only online.
5. BCite, Bloomberg Law's citator, is available only online.

Sometimes you will not have an applicable statute or a relevant secondary source. In this situation, you will have to manufacture your own entry point into case law. To do this, you can search by subject in print or online or use a full-text search online.

B. Subject Searching in Print or Online

1. Subject Searching on Lexis Advance

Lexis Advance has subject searching tools that can be combined with its full-text search capabilities or used on their own. Lexis Advance editors assign each case headnotes that identify the main points of law in the case in the exact language the court uses. These headnotes appear before the text of the opinion.[6]

Searching by topic on Lexis Advance can be helpful when you have very little information about the area you are researching. To use this tool, click on the "Browse" tab on the home screen. The resulting screen lets you browse by "Sources," "Topics," or "Practice Pages." Choosing "Topics" allows you to search for a topic with words or phrases or explore the topics listed there. If, for example, you click on "Torts," the resulting screen displays an expandable hierarchy in which you can open "Intentional Torts" to arrive at "Intentional Infliction of Emotional Distress," which can be expanded to show "General Overview," "Defenses," "Elements," and "Remedies." Clicking on "Elements" allows you to search one of two ways. First, you may retrieve a list of all cases to which the editors have assigned that topic. You may then further filter that list and search the list using terms and connectors. Second, you may add that topic as a search filter and run a search. Figure 5-1 shows an example of browsing the Lexis Advance Topics.

You can also enter the topic system by using the headnote from a relevant case, if you have one. In the "LexisNexis Headnotes" section of the case, find an appropriate topic or subtopic in a relevant headnote, and then click the topic or subtopic. You may then retrieve a list of authorities to which the editors have assigned that topic or subtopic. In addition, you may use *Shepard's* to retrieve a list of authorities citing the case for the proposition contained in the relevant headnote. Figure 5-2 shows an example of the topics and subtopics listed in the headnotes of a case on Lexis Advance.

---

6. You can show or hide headnotes in the Lexis Advance display of a case.

Figure 5-1. Lexis Advance Browsing by Topic

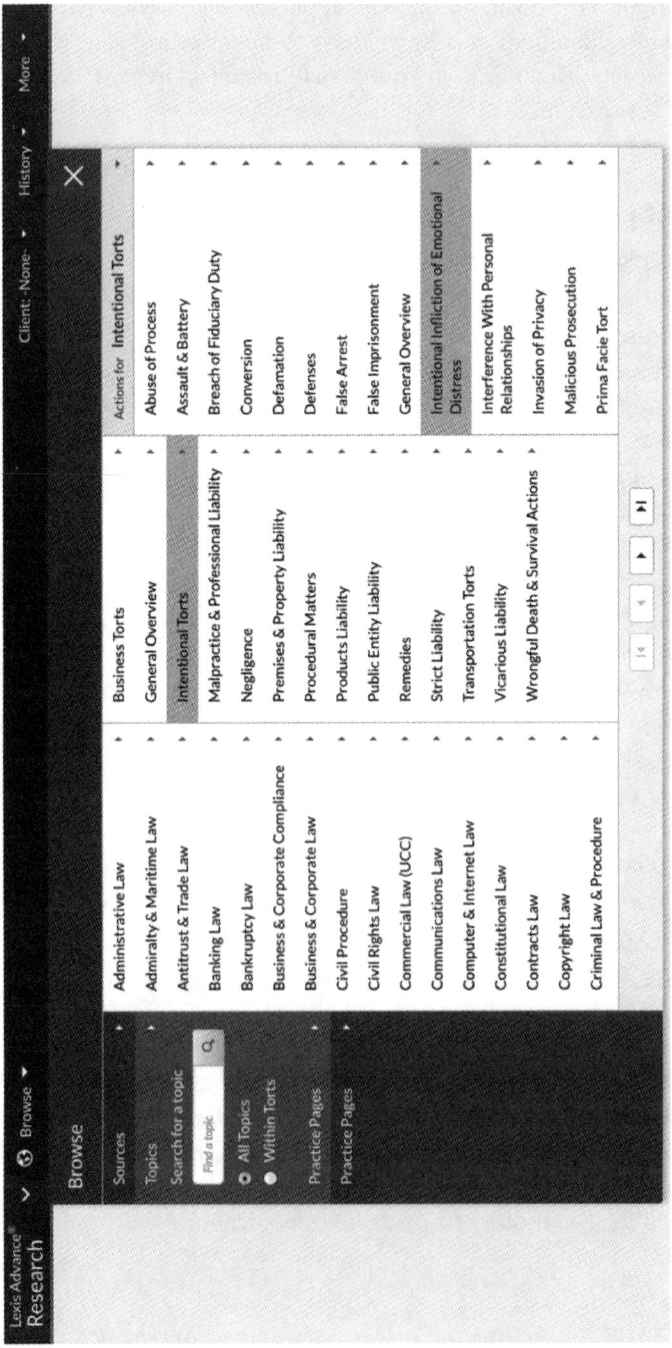

Source: Lexis Advance. Used with permission of LexisNexis.

Figure 5-2. LexisNexis Headnotes

▼ LexisNexis® Headnotes

Torts > Intentional Torts ▼ > ▓ False Imprisonment ▼ > General Overview ▼

HN1 If a man is restrained of his personal liberty by fear of a personal difficulty, that amounts to a false imprisonment within the legal meaning of such term. *Shepardize* - Narrow by this Headnote

Labor & Employment Law > Employment Relationships ▼ > ▓ At Will Employment ▼ > General Overview ▼

Torts > Intentional Torts ▼ > ▓ False Imprisonment ▼ > General Overview ▼

HN2 A plaintiff who relinquishes his right to move about freely as the only available alternative to relinquishment of another right, such as the right to an unsullied reputation, is restrained, or imprisoned, in the sense that imprisonment is an element of tortious false imprisonment. That is the type of restraint by fear of personal difficulty to which the court referred in those cases. But an employee at will who relinquishes his right to move about in return for continued employment, to which he is not entitled, is not imprisoned. He has a free choice. *Shepardize* - Narrow by this Headnote

Source: Lexis Advance. Used with permission of LexisNexis.

2. Subject Searching in West: The Key Number System

West has a comprehensive system of subject searching called the "Key Number System." In print, West uses this system to provide subject access to cases in its print reporters through tools called "digests." The Key Number System is also a feature of Westlaw.

The Key Number System is an extensive outline of the law. It uses "topics," which are broad classifications, and "key numbers," which are subheadings within the broad classifications.

The system is built on the foundation of headnotes, in which West editors summarize the points of law in a case.[7] Some cases have many headnotes; others have relatively few. The *Bortolotti* case, excerpted at Figure 4-4 in a West reporter, has eleven West headnotes.

A headnote is a very brief distillation, by a West editor, of a point of law in a case. Each headnote is assigned a topic and key number from the outline of the law developed by West. When you look up a topic and key number in a print digest or on Westlaw, you find "blurbs" or "squibs" of cases classified under that topic and key number. Each gives the text of a headnote and the citation to the case from which the headnote came. Since the Key Number System allows you to gather cases that deal with a particular point of law, the system is in effect an index to case law.

a. West Digests

West publishes regional digests that correspond to four of its regional reporters: Atlantic, North Western, Pacific, and Southeastern. Regional digests generally have more than one series.[8] West also publishes digests for all states except Delaware, Nevada, and Utah. In addition, West publishes digests for the federal courts in general and specifically for the Supreme Court. West's digest system includes the *Decennial Digest*, which includes cases from throughout the U.S.[9]

---

7. Headnotes appear at the beginning of reports of decisions in print West reporters and on Westlaw in the order in which the points are addressed in the case.

8. Digest series are not cumulative. Thus, when researching in print, you may need to refer to more than one series of a digest to make sure that your digest search covers the relevant period. The series designation of a regional digest does not necessarily correspond to the series designation of the regional reporter.

9. Once published at ten-year intervals, the *Decennial Digest* is now published more frequently. The Twelfth Series of the *Decennial Digest* has, to date, two parts. Part II was published in 2014.

The topic and key number system is uniform across all West digests.[10] There- fore, if you are working with a topic and key number in the *Massachusetts Digest* and want to find New Hampshire cases on the same topic, you can look up the same topic and key number in the *Atlantic Digest* or the *New Hampshire Digest*.

b. Using the Key Number System

For a print digest search, your first decision is which digest to use. In gen- eral, it is most efficient to use the narrowest digest, that is, the digest that in- cludes headnotes of cases from the fewest jurisdictions. For example, if you know that you are looking for cases only from Massachusetts, the *Massachusetts Digest* would be your best choice because it does not include headnotes of cases from other states.[11] On Westlaw, there is no need to select a digest. The Key Number System on Westlaw allows you to select the jurisdictions in which you are interested.

1. Locating Relevant Topics and Key Numbers

Both in print and on Westlaw, there are several ways to find topics and key numbers that will lead you to potentially relevant cases. These are the case method, the descriptive-word method, and the topic method.

a. Case Method

If you have the citation to a relevant case, looking up that case in a print West reporter or on Westlaw gets you its topics and key numbers. Looking up relevant topics and key numbers in a digest or locating them on Westlaw leads you to headnotes of (and citations to) other potentially relevant cases. Thus, if you are working on a problem that includes an issue on the rule against perpetuities, a topic in the law of Property, headnotes in the *Bortolotti* case would lead you to relevant topics and key numbers, and thus to other potentially relevant cases.

b. Descriptive-Word Method

If you do not have a case in hand, the descriptive-word method is an effective way to find potentially relevant topics and key numbers. Like the case method, you can use this method in print or on Westlaw.

In print, use the Descriptive-Word Index (DWI) volumes that are shelved near the end of a digest set. Generate terms for searching the DWI through

---

10. Westlaw uses the same system.

11. The *Massachusetts Digest* also includes cases originating in Massachusetts federal courts. To expand your digest search beyond Massachusetts, you would have to use the *Decennial Digest*. There is no digest that corresponds to the *North Eastern Reporter*.

the kind of organized brainstorming described in Chapter 2 (by reflecting on the issue or asking yourself standard questions using the journalistic approach or the TARPP approach). Looking up a number of different search words in the DWI will likely help you triangulate your key number search by leading you to several topics and key numbers—with the most relevant topics and key numbers coming up multiple times.

Like many print legal resources, digest volumes, including DWI volumes, are updated periodically with pocket parts. When you search the DWI, flip to the back of each volume you consult to check the pocket part. Also check both main volumes and pocket parts when you follow up on the topics and key numbers you locate in your DWI search.

Westlaw has a key number search feature that can be used in a manner similar to the DWI. To use this feature, click on the "Tools" tab at the top of the home screen, and then click "West Key Number System." You may then perform a terms-and-connectors search of the entire West Key Number System. Click the key number itself to find headnotes to which the West editors have assigned that key number. Westlaw lets you limit your results to particular jurisdictions.

c. Topic Method

Finally, you can use the topic method to search for topics and key numbers. This method assumes some familiarity with legal categories in general and with the West classification system in particular. For that reason, this method is generally less effective than others for new legal researchers. Even experienced researchers are sometimes surprised by what is included or excluded under a given topic.

To search by topic in a print digest, peruse the spines of the digest volumes arrayed on your library shelf and choose the volume that has what you think is the most promising topic. Open the volume to the beginning of that topic and skim the summary of contents or the outline until you find a key number entry that seems appropriate to follow up. Turn to the corresponding key number and read the headnotes collected there.

On Westlaw, pull up the West Key Number System as described in subsection b. above. This tool allows you to browse through the topics at the most general level or to expand them to reach the level of key numbers. Click the desired key number to see a list of headnotes assigned to that key number, and limit your results by jurisdiction as needed.

2. Working with Headnotes

After finding promising topics and key numbers, you must look them up to see where they lead. If you are using a print digest, go to the appropriate volume of the digest, look up the topic and key number, and look over the headnotes. If the cases seem relevant, then you are probably in the right place (or in one of the right places). If you are in a digest that includes headnotes from more than one jurisdiction, make sure you distinguish between cases that are mandatory authority for your problem and those that are not.

Figure 5-3 is a short excerpt from a *Decennial Digest* that shows some of the headnotes grouped under the topic "Contracts" and the key number 116(1). Figure 5-4 shows two of the forty-three headnotes grouped under 95k116(1) in Westlaw, corresponding to Contracts 116(1).

Westlaw offers many ways to follow up a promising topic and key number combination. First, clicking on the relevant key number retrieves a browsable list of headnotes, similar to what you would find under a topic and key number in a print digest. Second, you may use the search bar to perform a natural-language or terms-and-connectors search of the headnotes. Third, you can construct a terms-and-connectors search in a case law source,[12] discussed below, that includes as terms the topics and key numbers that you are interested in pursuing. In this type of search, you must use the numerical designation of the topic, which you can find in the online West Key Number System.

3. Updating Print Digests

Working in a print digest requires a step not needed for subject searching on Westlaw: updating. The physical realities of print publishing require that a print volume cut off at a particular point in time so it can be printed and distributed. A volume of a print digest obviously does not include cases decided after the cut-off point. To update a digest search, first check the pocket part of each main volume. Then check any supplement published after the most recent pocket part. Finally, check the mini-digest within each West advance sheet and reporter volume published after the last supplement to the digest. Using this method, a researcher can update a digest research to a point that is quite close to the present.

Although updating in print is feasible, it is a cumbersome process to pull multiple advance sheets and reporters from library shelves to check the mini-

---

12. Lexis Advance and Bloomberg Law call their sets of materials "sources"; Westlaw calls them "content categories." For ease of reference, we will use the term "sources" when referring to the specific types of material you will search.

Figure 5-3. Excerpt from Contracts 116(1) in *Decennial Digest*

14 11th D Pt 1—933

CONTRACTS ⟨⟩116(1)

La.App. 4 Cir. 1997. Agreement limiting competition must strictly comply with requirements of statute. LSA–R.S. 23:921.—Dixie Parking Service, Inc. v. Hargrove, 691 So.2d 1316, 96-1929 (La.App. 4 Cir. 3/26/97).

La.App. 5 Cir. 1996. Louisiana has strong public policy against noncompetition agreements.—Millet v. Crump, 687 So.2d 132, 96-639 (La.App. 5 Cir. 12/30/96), rehearing denied.

Mass. 1997. Noncompetition agreements between employers and former employees are generally enforceable to extent they are reasonable.—Pettingell v. Morrison, Mahoney & Miller, 687 N.E.2d 1237, 426 Mass. 253.

Minn. 1998. Employment noncompete agreements are looked upon with disfavor, cautiously considered, and carefully scrutinized.—Kallok v. Medtronic, Inc., 573 N.W.2d 356, rehearing denied.

Noncompete agreements are enforceable if they serve legitimate employer interest and are not broader than necessary to protect this interest.—Id.

Restrictive covenants limiting individuals in the exercise or pursuit of their occupations are in restraint of trade.—Id.

Post-employment restrictions are generally considered restraints of trade.—Id.

The purpose of the restrictive covenant is to protect an employer from unfair competition.—Id.

The employee owes his relationship with the client to the employer, and he holds the relationship in a kind of fiduciary capacity for the employer, and thus, it is perfectly fair, for a limited time after the termination of the employment, to prohibit his using that relationship for his own benefit and for the benefit of a competitor of the employer, to the employer's detriment.—Id.

Mo.App. E.D. 1999. A covenant not to compete must be reasonable in scope as to geography and time and must be reasonably necessary to protect certain narrowly defined and well-recognized employer interests.—Washington County Memorial Hosp. v. Sidebottom, 7 S.W.3d 542.

Noncompete agreements emanate from purpose of protecting business entity from unfair competition by former business associate without imposing unreasonable restraints on the latter.—Id.

Promises imposing restraints on exercise of trade or calling that are ancillary to valid transaction or relationship, and that thus may be valid if reasonable in scope and duration, include employer-employee and buyer-seller relationships and partners against partnerships; however, this is not an exclusive list, and there may be other situations in which valid transaction or relationship would give promisee legitimate interest sufficient to sustain promise not to compete. Restatement (Second) of Contracts § 188.—Id.

Noncompete agreements are not favored in the law.—Id.

Mo.App. E.D. 1996. Purpose of covenant not to compete is not to punish employees, but to protect employers from unfair competition by former employees without imposing unreasonable restraint on employees.—Sturgis Equipment Co., Inc. v. Falcon Indus. Sales Co., 930 S.W.2d 14, rehearing, transfer denied (681001), and transfer

Source: 14 *Eleventh Decennial Digest, Part 1* Contracts 116(1) (2001). Reprinted with permission of Thomson Reuters.

Figure 5-4. Headnotes Under 95k116(1) in Westlaw

(1) In general (65) ☆ Add to Favorites

Jurisdiction: 1st Circuit Change

Sort by: [Topic then Date ↕]   🖼 ▼

1 - 50 ▲

☐ Select all items | No items selected

95 CONTRACTS 6,307
— 95I Requisites and Validity 2,190
—— 95I(F) Legality of Object and of Consideration 953
———— 95⟶115 Restraint of Trade or Competition in Trade 175
—————— 95⟶116 In General 112
———————— 95⟶116(1) In general. 65

☐ **1. 7-Eleven, Inc. v. Grewal**

United States District Court, D. Massachusetts. | November 20, 2014 | --- F.Supp.3d ----

Headnote: Under Massachusetts law, a covenant not to compete is enforceable only if it is necessary to protect a legitimate business interest, it is reasonably limited in time and space, and it is consonant with the public interest.

Document Preview: Background: Convenience store franchisor brought action against franchisee, seeking injunctive relief and monetary damages, relating to alleged violation of franchise agreement's non-compete clause and alleged trademark infringement after termination of franchise. Parties filed cross-motions for preliminary injunction. **Holdings:** The District Court, Mastroianni, J., held that: 5(1) franchisor was likely to succeed on merits of trademark infringement claim; but 21(2) franchisor would not suffer irreparable harm in absence of preliminary injunction to enforce non-compete clause; and 22(3) balancing of harms did not favor preliminary injunction to enforce non-compete clause.   Franchisor's motion granted in part and denied in part; franchisee's motion denied.

☐ **2. Outside Television, Inc. v. Murin**

United States District Court, D. Maine. | October 10, 2013 | 977 F.Supp.2d 1

Headnote: Under Maine law, non-competition covenants will be enforced only to the extent that they are reasonable and sweep no wider than necessary to protect the business interests in issue.

Document Preview: LITIGATION - Injunction. Television broadcaster seeking preliminary injunction against former employee was not likely to succeed on the merits.

digest in each. Thus, most researchers who have access to Westlaw update their digest search online, by looking up promising topics and key numbers to check for cases decided after the close of the print volume or most recent cumulative supplement.

3. Subject Searching in Bloomberg Law

Bloomberg Law offers limited topic searching in a few areas through its Practice Centers. The ten Practice Centers currently offered are Antitrust, Banking & Finance, Bankruptcy, Corporate/Mergers & Acquisitions, Employee Benefits, Health, Intellectual Property, Labor & Employment, Securities, and Tax. Choose your "Practice Centers" and then select "Opinions & Dockets" to search cases within that Practice Center. A few Practice Centers (e.g., Employee Benefits and Labor & Employment) offer hierarchies of topics and subtopics that allow you to browse case summaries, similar to the Lexis Advance Topics and the West Key Number System. The other Practice Centers allow terms-and-connectors searching of cases relevant to the selected practice areas, rather than browsing case summaries by subject.

C. Full-Text Searching in Commercial Research Services

Many commercial research services allow the legal researcher to retrieve relevant cases by searching for words within them.[13] Lexis Advance and Westlaw allow you to locate cases by natural-language or terms-and-connectors searching. Bloomberg Law offers terms-and-connectors, but not natural-language, search capability. Researchers may also use natural-language searches to find cases on Google Scholar.

Most researchers are familiar with natural-language searching through non-legal research. In this form of searching, you simply enter words that you think will occur in the material you are searching for. The commercial research service then applies its own programmed logic to identify and rank the words in your query, runs the search, and gives you the results. Terms-and-connectors searching is more technical because it requires you to make predictions about the precise language and syntax of the authorities you seek. It may, however, yield more precise results than natural-language searching does.

---

13. Services that offer full-text searching include Bloomberg Law, Casemaker, Fastcase, Lexis Advance, Ravel Law, and Westlaw. Appendix A describes techniques for constructing full-text searches.

1. Choosing an Appropriate Source

Choosing appropriate sources is the essential first step in conducting a full-text search on a commercial research service. These services retrieve materials only from the places you tell them to look. Thus, if you are looking for cases decided by Massachusetts courts, you must search in a source that contains Massachusetts cases.

Commercial research services let you choose what type of material to search (i.e., cases or statutes). For case law research, you might specify one or more jurisdictions relevant to your problem in order to yield the most useful search results. The leading services allow you to limit your search to particular jurisdictions and to specific sets of materials within those jurisdictions. For example, you could limit your search to all Massachusetts cases, or just to cases from the Supreme Judicial Court.

a. Choosing a Source on Lexis Advance

Lexis Advance offers several ways to choose a source. First, you can use the "Explore Content" tab to browse for relevant sources. For example, if you select "State" and then "Massachusetts," you find a list of Massachusetts-specific sources organized by type of source, such as cases, statutes, administrative materials, secondary materials, and more. Figure 5-5 shows the "Cases" section of the Massachusetts-specific sources available through the Explore Content tab. Second, you can use the "Filters" button to limit your search by jurisdiction, type of authority, and practice area. Third, you may use the "Browse" tab and then select "Sources." From there, you can search for a specific source if you already know the source you want to search, or you can browse through possible sources as in the Explore Content tab. When you find a source for your search, add it as a filter and then run your search. Finally, as you type a search in the search bar, Lexis Advance may suggest sources for your search in a drop-down menu.

b. Choosing a Source on Westlaw

Westlaw offers several ways to choose a source. First, you can use the "Jurisdiction" button to select one or more jurisdictions. Then run your search in the search bar. Second, you can type terms into the search bar, and Westlaw will show you suggested sources. Select the desired source and run your search in the search bar. Third, you can use the "Browse" section of the home page to find a relevant source. For example, if you select "State Materials" and then "Massachusetts," you will have a menu of Massachusetts sources to choose, as shown in Figure 5-6. Select your source and run your search in the search bar.

Figure 5-5. Browsing for Massachusetts Sources on Lexis Advance

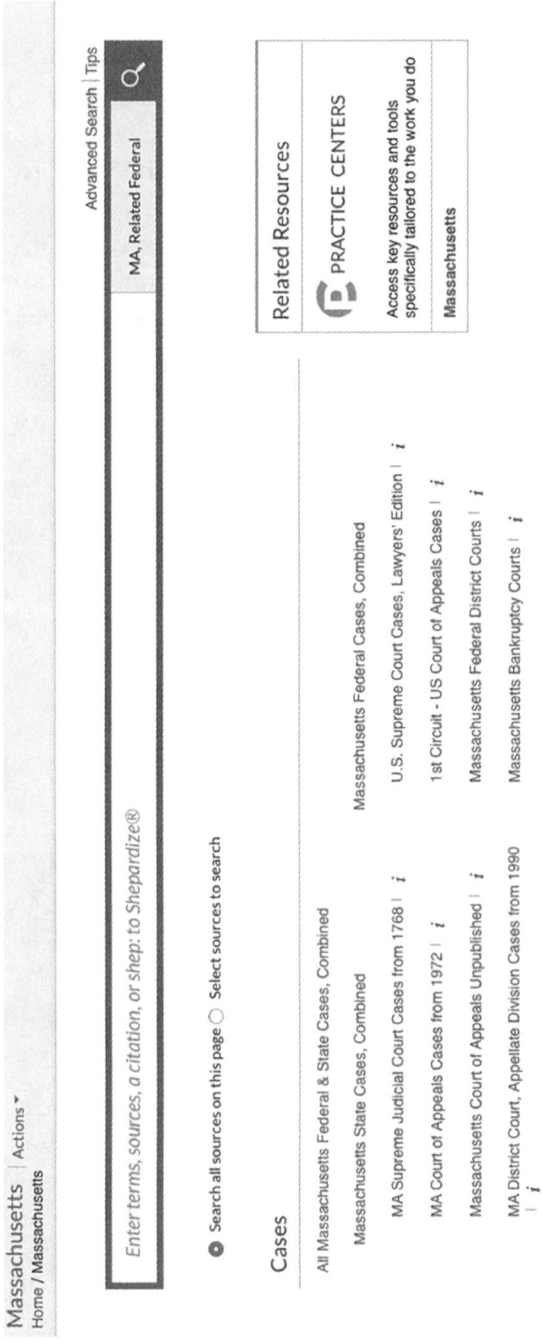

Massachusetts | Actions ▼
Home / Massachusetts

Advanced Search | Tips

Enter terms, sources, a citation, or shep: to Shepardize®

MA, Related Federal

🔍

◉ Search all sources on this page ○ Select sources to search

Cases

All Massachusetts Federal & State Cases, Combined

Massachusetts State Cases, Combined

MA Supreme Judicial Court Cases from 1768 | *i*

MA Court of Appeals Cases from 1972 | *i*

Massachusetts Court of Appeals Unpublished | *i*

MA District Court, Appellate Division Cases from 1990 | *i*

MA Superior Court Cases from 1993 | *i*

Massachusetts Land Court | *i*

Massachusetts Federal Cases, Combined

U.S. Supreme Court Cases, Lawyers' Edition | *i*

1st Circuit - US Court of Appeals Cases | *i*

Massachusetts Federal District Courts | *i*

Massachusetts Bankruptcy Courts | *i*

Related Resources

Ⓟ PRACTICE CENTERS

Access key resources and tools
specifically tailored to the work you do

Massachusetts

Source: Lexis Advance. Used with permission of LexisNexis.

Figure 5-6. Browsing for Massachusetts Sources on Westlaw

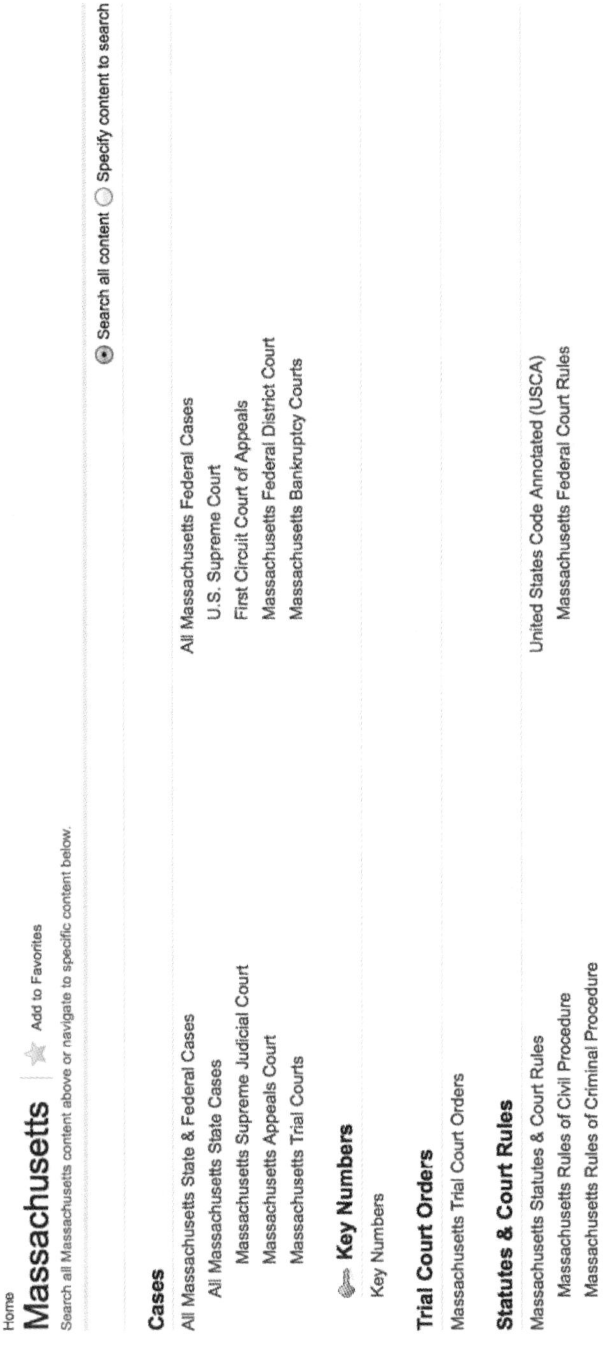
Home
Massachusetts
Add to Favorites
Search all Massachusetts content above or navigate to specific content below.
Search all content
Specify content to search
Cases
All Massachusetts State & Federal Cases
All Massachusetts State Cases
Massachusetts Supreme Judicial Court
Massachusetts Appeals Court
Massachusetts Trial Courts
All Massachusetts Federal Cases
U.S. Supreme Court
First Circuit Court of Appeals
Massachusetts Federal District Court
Massachusetts Bankruptcy Courts
Key Numbers
Key Numbers
Trial Court Orders
Massachusetts Trial Court Orders
Statutes & Court Rules
Massachusetts Statutes & Court Rules
Massachusetts Rules of Civil Procedure
Massachusetts Rules of Criminal Procedure
United States Code Annotated (USCA)
Massachusetts Federal Court Rules

Source: Westlaw. Used with permission of Thomson Reuters.

c. Choosing a Source on Bloomberg Law

To select a source on Bloomberg Law, select "Search & Browse" and then select "Court Opinions." You may then browse through sources for particular state cases, federal cases, or state and federal combined cases. For example, you can expand the "State Opinions" source to see a list of all states. Then select "Massachusetts" to see the available sources for Massachusetts cases. Click each source in which you want to run your search. The selected sources appear below the hierarchy of sources, as shown in Figure 5-7.

Figure 5-7. Browsing for Massachusetts Sources on Bloomberg Law

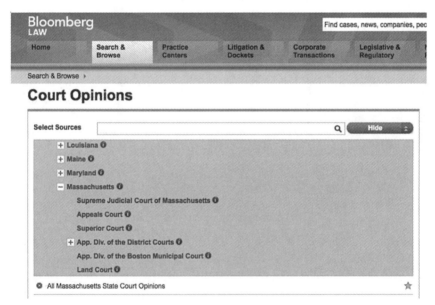

2. Constructing a Natural-Language Search

Natural-language searching on Lexis Advance or Westlaw uses regular conversational English to request information. Most researchers are familiar with natural-language searching because it is the main way we search the web. A natural-language search on Lexis Advance or Westlaw can be a string of words or a question. Appendix B discusses how to construct a natural-language search.[14]

3. Constructing a Terms-and-Connectors Search

Terms-and-connectors searching is a powerful tool for searching online sources. This type of searching relies on the researcher specifying relationships among search terms to generate precise results. Lexis Advance, Westlaw, and Bloomberg Law give you many options to help you construct precise terms-and-connectors searches. As with natural-language searching, you must select an appropriate source in which to search.

Terms-and-connectors searching is more technical than the natural-language searching you may be accustomed to using on Google or other internet search engines. A terms-and-connectors search will retrieve exactly what it is instructed to retrieve, so an imperfectly constructed search may produce a result that is too broad or too narrow—or even produce a result that is not at all what you were searching for. To produce effective terms-and-connectors searches, study carefully the rules that the commercial research services prescribe for using connectors and other Boolean tools and take any opportunity you have for free online tutorials or practice sessions. Appendix B discusses how to construct a terms-and-connectors search.

III. Additional Case Law Research Tasks

Whatever techniques you use to assemble a group of potentially relevant cases, you will need to perform three additional research tasks before you can be reasonably certain that you have found the group of cases that together are the body of authority that applies to your client's problem.[15] You will need to 1) evaluate your initial result list, 2) expand your result list to include other cases that you might not have picked up in your initial research, and 3) validate the cases on which you plan to rely to make sure they are good law.

---

14. Both systems also offer options for restricting the search to obtain a more focused result.

15. This statement assumes that you have ascertained that there are no constitutional provisions, statutes, regulations, or other administrative materials that apply to your client's problem. (See Chapter 1 on the hierarchy of authority.)

A. Evaluating Your Initial Result List

While you could try to collect every possibly relevant authority before reading any of them, reading and analyzing cases in stages is generally more efficient. This approach gives you the opportunity to reflect on what you have found before you invest a great deal of time and energy in following a path that might not yield fruitful results. The most effective process for working on a case law problem is to begin with cases that identify the general principles of law and policy that apply to the problem. Once you are confident that you have a grasp of the big picture, move on to identify specific cases that are factually similar to your problem.

1. Reading a Few Recent Cases

To get an accurate understanding of the current status of the law, begin with recent cases in the general area of law you are researching. Recent cases in an area will incorporate developments in the law and cite the authority on which they rely. If the most recent case in a jurisdiction is from the intermediate appellate court, consider starting there. Your goal at this point is to get a general picture of the overall structure of the courts' analysis, so it is not necessary to start with a case from the highest court in the jurisdiction. Of course, if you are relying on a case from an intermediate appellate court, you will need to assure yourself that the reasoning in that opinion is consistent with the reasoning of the highest appellate court.

Reading a small group of recent cases early in your research process will not only help you grasp the overall structure of the analysis. This step will also lead you to other relevant cases because courts cite the authority on which they rely. Moreover, reading a few recent cases will help you begin to grasp the range of fact patterns that arise in this area of law. This understanding will help you make initial judgments about which facts are legally significant and suggest lines of further factual research and ways to narrow your initial result list.

2. Identifying Factually Similar Cases

Once you understand the overall structure of the analysis, you are ready to dig into the result list you compiled originally, as expanded by any additional potentially relevant cases you came across as you read the cases on your list. At this point, your goal will be to identify more specifically the issues raised by your client's problem. Here, you will likely focus on identifying and reading factually similar cases.

B. Expanding Your Research to Identify Additional Relevant Cases

Experienced legal researchers agree that in most situations your initial result list should not set the boundaries of your research. This is because any one research tool or technique may not yield complete and accurate results for a given problem. This "deficiency" may result from the coverage of the tool or the way you use it. Thus, when you are searching for relevant cases, use methods to expand your research to locate relevant cases that, for whatever reason, did not turn up in your initial result list.

There are two main ways to expand your research. First, as discussed above, you can expand your initial result list by reading cases cited by relevant cases on that list. Second, you can expand your research by using a method different from the method you used to compile your initial result list. Some experienced legal researchers recommend using more than one method so that you can triangulate your research: by using two or three different methods, you are likely to pick up most, if not all, of the cases you might miss with just one method.

This chapter discusses two main methods to compile an initial result list. The first is subject searching on Lexis Advance or using the West Key Number System in the print digest or on Westlaw. These methods do not search the full text of cases, but rather lead you to editorial features that are similar to indexes, which then lead you to cases. The second method is full-text searching, by natural-language or terms-and-connectors, in case law sources on Lexis Advance, Westlaw, or Bloomberg Law. Each commercial research service uses its own search algorithm, and therefore may find different material. Moreover, variation in the way you construct your searches may lead you to cases that you did not find by another method.

A third method to expand your research is to use a legal citator: *Shepard's* on Lexis Advance, KeyCite on Westlaw, or BCite on Bloomberg Law.[16] These services are designed primarily to permit researchers to validate their research by pointing to virtually all later sources that cite an authority, thereby allowing the researcher to determine whether and how later sources have affected the authority on which the researcher proposes to rely.[17] Using citators to validate

---

16. Chapter 2 introduces citators. Print *Shepard's* are available, but are not as current or easy to use as online citators.

17. *Shepard's* and KeyCite are not limited to cases. You can use them to validate primary authority other than cases and some secondary authority, and to expand research in both primary and secondary authority. BCite is currently limited to cases.

your research is discussed below. Because citators point to sources that cite to a given authority, they provide the researcher with another tool for expanding research. By using a citator, you can locate all cases that have cited a case that you have determined is relevant. A case that cites that relevant case may also be relevant to your research.

To use *Shepard's*, KeyCite, or BCite to expand your case law research, use cases that you have identified as "leading" cases (that is, the cases that other cases in this area tend to cite) or otherwise are central to the specific problem you are researching. For example, if you are working on a problem involving enforceability of a prenuptial agreement and decide that *Osborne v. Osborne*, 384 Mass. 591 (1981), is a leading case, you can use that case to expand your research to find later, relevant cases.

On each of the services, you see preliminary citator information when you pull up a case. When trying to expand your research, you should select all of the cases that cite your leading case and then narrow your results to the relevant jurisdiction. You can narrow your results by type of authority, such as cases or secondary sources, by jurisdiction, by topic or headnote, by date, or (on *Shepard's* and KeyCite) by the depth in which the authorities discuss your case. These filters make a citator a powerful and efficient tool for expanding your search results efficiently.

C. Validating the Cases

At points in your research you will need to validate your findings. Validation is essential in any research project because a judicial opinion may affect a previously decided case, for example, by overruling, reversing, or distinguishing it. Thus, a case on which you propose to rely may not be "good law," in other words, not valid precedent. Even if the case has not been reversed or explicitly overruled, it may have been distinguished by later cases to the extent that it is much weaker authority for a given assertion than it was before the later cases were decided.

Like so many research tasks, validating your research is not something you should save for the end of a project. Rather, it is a task that you should do as you go along in order to avoid the risk of basing analysis on invalid or on weakened authority.

Citators make this task relatively easy because you can see immediately from the report of a case whether it has been negatively affected. If the case has significant negative history, you will see the service's warning symbol—yellow for some negative history and red for significant negative history.[18] Click the symbol to see cases that treated your case negatively.[19] Then validate the case fully by learning precisely how the citing case negatively affected the case you are validating. The information provided by citator symbols alone is insufficient for purposes of determining whether the case remains valid for the precise point of law on which you propose to rely. Think of the symbols not as definitive, but rather as indications that further exploration is in order. You must skim or read the citing case itself in order to understand precisely how the citing case affected the case you are validating.

D. Deciding When Your Case Law Research Is Complete

Integrating the operations discussed in this chapter requires you to reflect on your research problem as you go along. Thus, if you read, analyze, and validate cases at every stage of the research process, you should not find it difficult to decide when your research is complete. At some point in your research, either a clear answer will take shape, or you will see that there is no clear answer and that you have to draw conclusions based on a less solid foundation.

With some problems, this point comes sooner than with others. When it comes depends on a number of factors, including how many authorities bear on your problem and whether the area of law is one that is fast-developing or one that is relatively settled.

One sign that your research is complete is when different methods yield no new cases. This sign may not be reliable, however, especially when you are researching in an area of law that is developing quickly. In general, however, triangulating your research and reading and reflecting as you go along will help decide when your case law research is complete.

---

18. See Figures 2-2, 2-3, and 2-4 for each service's citator symbols.
19. Each service's citator also lets you choose whether to view just the direct history of your case, just the negative history, or all of the authorities that cite your case.

Chapter 6

Statutes

I. Introduction

A statute is law that is enacted by a legislature. A statute is primary authority that is binding within the jurisdiction of the legislature that enacts it. The United States Congress enacts federal statutes, which are binding authority throughout the United States. A state legislature enacts state statutes, which are binding authority throughout that state.[1] Since colonial times, when the Massachusetts legislature had judicial as well as legislative powers, the official name of the Massachusetts legislature has been the "General Court."

Today, very few areas of law remain governed wholly by case law. If a statute applies, the text of the statute, rather than a case, is the appropriate starting point for analysis. While courts apply and interpret statutes, they cannot change or disregard them. In contrast, by enacting a statute, a legislature can change a legal principle grounded in case law or create new legal principles, so long as the legislation is consistent with the relevant state constitution and the Constitution of the United States. Thus, when you strategize your research on a problem, always look first for an applicable statute.

Although statutes and cases are both primary authority, they are created and published differently. Thus, the sources and some of the techniques you use to research statutory law differ from those you use to research case law.

---

1. The legislative body of a municipality also has power to enact law. In Massachusetts, law enacted by a City Council or Board of Aldermen is referred to as an "ordinance." Law enacted by the legislative body of a town, for example by a Town Meeting or by a Board of Selectman, is referred to as a "by-law."

II. How Statutes Are Published

While the U.S. Congress and each state has its own specific legislative process,[2] their statutes are published according to the same general pattern. In general, statutes are first printed as individual documents called "slip laws." The laws of each session of the legislature are collected chronologically into publications called "session laws." Then, the permanent laws of general applicability[3] are codified, that is, arranged into topical compilations of statutes called "codes."

For most research projects, a code has distinct advantages for the legal researcher over a compilation of session laws.[4] First, codes are arranged by topic, instead of by date of enactment, so related statutes are grouped together. Second, unlike compilations of session laws, codes remove repealed or expired provisions and incorporate amendments. Third, many codes are annotated.

An annotated code includes valuable aids for the legal researcher, including "credits." Credits are citations to historical material that shows when a given section of a statute was first enacted and later legislation affecting the section. An annotated code provides references to relevant legislative history and administrative regulations. It also includes references to secondary sources and practice materials. Particularly useful features of an annotated code are summaries of decisions applying or interpreting the statute. Figure 6-1 shows a section of the Massachusetts code, with some of its annotations, from *Annotated Laws of Massachusetts*, a print publication. Figure 6-2 shows the same section, with excerpts from its annotations, as published electronically on Lexis Advance.

---

2. For a detailed description of Massachusetts legislative procedure, see Chapter 3 of *Handbook of Legal Research in Massachusetts* (Mary Ann Neary & Ruth Matz eds., 3d ed., Mass. CLE 2009 & Supps. 2012 & 2015).

3. Some laws enacted by a legislature are of limited applicability. For example, the U.S. Congress may enact special legislation naming a federal building. In Massachusetts, "special laws" are acts applying to a specific city, town, district, individual, or group of individuals.

4. The exception to this general rule is the situation in which a special law applies. Since codes include only general laws, a code is not a useful resource for a problem involving a special law.

Figure 6-1. Section of *Annotated Laws of Massachusetts* in Print

C. 208   ANNOTATED LAWS OF MASSACHUSETTS   **§ 33**

§ 33.   **Jurisdiction and Procedure Under This Chapter.**

text of statute

The court may, if the course of proceeding is not specially prescribed, hear and determine all matters coming within the purview of this chapter according to the course of proceedings in ecclesiastical courts or in courts of equity, and may issue process of attachment and execution and all other proper and necessary processes. In such proceedings the court shall have jurisdiction in equity of all causes cognizable under the general principles of equity jurisprudence, arising between husband and wife, such jurisdiction to be exercised in accordance with the usual course of practice in equity proceedings.

History—

credits

1785, 69, § 8; 1820, 56, § 1; RS 1836, 76, § 38; GS 1860, 107, § 53; PS 1882, 146, § 33; 1887, 332, § 1; RL 1902, 152, § 29; 1931, 426, § 95; 1936, 221, § 1.

Cross.References—

cross-reference to relevant code section

Awarding costs, ALM GL c 208 § 38.

Annotations—

Propriety of consideration of, and disposition as to, third persons' property claims in divorce litigation. 63 ALR3d 373.

Texts—

reference to secondary authority

Harvey, Moriarty, Bryant, *Massachusetts Domestic Relations*, 2d Ed. (Michie) § 51:2, Forms 204, 205.

Law Reviews—

ABC's of Massachusetts Divorce Practice and Procedure: Revised January 1, 1977. 21 Boston Bar J 6.

The doctrine of "clean hands" in Massachusetts annulment proceeding. 49 Mass LQ 235.

CASE NOTES

1. In general
2. Scope of powers conferred by section
3. Decree and execution

outline to summaries of cases interpreting the statue and first (and part of second) case summary

1. In general

The entry of a decree dismissing a libel for divorce often, and perhaps prima facie, means a decision on the merits. Wight v Wight (1930) 272 Mass 154, 172 NE 335.

Where wife commenced divorce proceeding in Ohio five days before husband filed complaint for divorce in Massachusetts Probate Court and Ohio court, having jurisdiction over marriage and husband, entered final judgment of divorce about three months before Massachusetts court entered judgment of divorce, Ohio judgment would be given full faith and credit, rendering Massachusetts judgment a nullity. Mannor v Mannor (1998) 46 Mass App 46, 703 NE2d 716.

2. Scope of powers conferred by section

Under this section, providing that the court might hear and determine all matters relating to divorce, according to the course of proceedings in ecclesiastical courts and in courts of chancery, the court was, in a suit for annulment, authorized to allow costs, unless there was something in the relation of husband and wife to pre-

166

Source: *Annotated Laws of Massachusetts*, Chapter 208, § 33 (Matthew Bender 2003). Matthew Bender is a registered trademark of Matthew Bender Properties Inc., a member of the LexisNexis Group. Used with permission of LexisNexis.

Figure 6-2. Section of *Annotated Laws of Massachusetts* on Lexis Advance

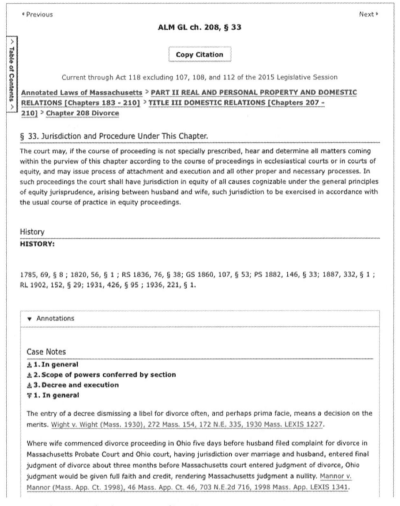

Source: Lexis Advance. Used with permission of LexisNexis.

III. Sources for Massachusetts Statutes

A. Print Sources

1. Session Laws

All the laws that the Massachusetts legislature enacts during each annual legislative session are compiled chronologically into a volume of the *Acts and*

Resolves of Massachusetts, the official version of the session laws.[5] There is no general index to the set of the *Acts and Resolves*, but each annual, bound volume includes a subject index covering the statutes within the volume as well as a table of code sections affected by the statutes included in the volume. Acts and resolves[6] are numbered chronologically, for example, as Chapter 5 of the Acts of 2008, which is cited as 2008 Mass. Acts 5.[7]

2. Official, Unannotated Code

The official Massachusetts code is an unannotated code called the *General Laws of Massachusetts*. Although the code is organized by title, chapter, and section, a provision is cited only by chapter and section, for example, as Mass. Gen. Laws ch. 93A, § 11.

The set of the *General Laws of Massachusetts* has eighteen volumes. The first fourteen volumes include laws; volumes fifteen through eighteen include a general index and a popular name table.[8] In addition to publishing laws, volume 1 begins with the Constitution of the United States followed by two versions of the Constitution of the Commonwealth of Massachusetts, one that integrates amendments and one that presents the constitution as originally enacted. This volume includes separate indexes to both the United States and Massachusetts constitutions.

The official code is republished every two years to integrate amendments enacted during the preceding two-year period.[9] For example, the 2014 edition

---

5. LexisNexis and West both publish unofficial versions of the Massachusetts session laws in print, with updating pamphlets.

6. A "resolve" is different from an "act" in that a resolve is generally not permanent legislation. Subjects of resolves include expressions of opinion, appointments of special committees, and ratifications of acts of public officials. *See* Louis Adams Frothingham, *A Brief History of the Constitution and Government of Massachusetts* 118 (Harvard U. 1916).

7. 2008 Mass. Acts 5 is a special act entitled "An Act Removing an Agricultural Restriction District in the Town of Raynham Known as the Borden Colony."

8. In a popular name table, statutes are indexed by their popular names. For example, you could look up "Lemon Law" without knowing that the initial act was Chapter 635 of the Acts and Resolves of 1970, "An Act authorizing the Voiding of Certain Motor Vehicle Contracts of Sale by the Buyer If Said Motor Vehicle Cannot Pass the Inspection Sticker Test."

9. Massachusetts statutes were recodified in 1921 as the "General Laws of 1921," when the entire code was enacted as a unit by the legislature to replace previous versions. The biennial editions of the official code are not revisions or recodifications, but rather republications that integrate changes to the code enacted by the legislature during the prior two-year period.

of the *General Laws* incorporates amendments enacted prior to January 1, 2015. During every two-year cycle, the *General Laws* is updated by monthly cumulative pamphlets that provide the text of session laws enacted through the month before the publication date of the pamphlet, as well as a table of code sections affected by those session laws.

3. Commercially Published, Annotated Codes

While the official Massachusetts code is unannotated, two commercial publishers publish unofficial, annotated print versions: *Massachusetts General Laws Annotated* (MGLA) and *Annotated Laws of Massachusetts* (ALM). These versions include valuable research aids, in addition to indexes.

Massachusetts General Laws Annotated (MGLA), published by West, contains the general laws in forty-nine volumes. These volumes are followed by several additional volumes that provide annotated versions of the United States and Massachusetts constitutions and court rules, as well as a general subject index and tables, including a popular name table. Within individual volumes, MGLA has separate subject indexes to some titles of the code.

MGLA volumes are updated with annual pocket parts, inserted into the back of individual volumes, which show changes enacted by the legislature to sections within those volumes and provide additional annotations. Between pocket parts, the set is updated at least once a year by an interim pamphlet that supplements the pocket parts by collating changes made by session laws with the affected code sections and updating annotations. Approximately monthly, West issues *Massachusetts Legislative Service* pamphlets. Each pamphlet provides the text of session laws enacted during the period covered by the pamphlet and includes a subject index as a well as several tables, including one that shows affected code sections.

Annotated Laws of Massachusetts (ALM) is the annotated version of the code published by LexisNexis. It includes the Massachusetts general laws in sixty-nine volumes. These volumes are followed by indexes and a popular name table. In separate volumes, ALM includes some, but not all, special laws. Additional volumes contain court rules and an annotated version of the Uniform Commercial Code as adopted by Massachusetts. Like MGLA volumes, ALM volumes are updated with cumulative pocket parts and interim updates, and with supplemental monthly pamphlets called *Advance Legislative Service*.

B. Online Sources

Massachusetts statutes, both the code and session laws, are available online through a number of sources. Some of these sources are free, while others are available only through commercial research services.

1. Free Internet Resources

Between the websites of the General Court and the State Library of Massachusetts, you can find free online versions of current and historical session laws, as well as an unofficial version of the *Massachusetts General Laws*. To date, there is no official online version of the *Massachusetts General Laws*.

a. Massachusetts Session Laws

The official website of the current session of the General Court contains the session laws back to 1997.[10] You can search the session laws by citation or keyword or browse by year.[11] For older session laws, the State Library maintains "DSpace," a free internet resource containing digital copies of the *Acts and Resolves* dating back to 1692.[12] DSpace lets you browse the *Acts and Resolves* by year.

b. Massachusetts Code

The website of the current session of the General Court contains an unofficial version of the code. This version is updated periodically to reflect changes to the general laws; it is searchable by citation or key words and browsable. Note, however, the prominent warning that this version is not official and that you should not rely on it without first checking an official version.

2. Commercial Research Services

a. Massachusetts Session Laws

Lexis Advance, Westlaw, and Bloomberg Law have sources containing session laws enacted in the current legislative session as well as recent legislative sessions. On Lexis Advance, the source "Massachusetts Advance Legislative Service" contains laws from the current session back to the 1990 session. On Westlaw, "Massachusetts Enacted Legislation (Session Laws)" contains laws from the current session and "Massachusetts Historical Enacted Legislation (Session Laws)" contains laws from sessions dating back to 1987. And on Bloomberg

---

10. The website is www.malegislature.gov. You can search and browse the acts separately from the resolves.

11. There is no index to the online version of the session laws.

12. The website is http://archives.lib.state.ma.us.

Law, the source "Massachusetts Session Laws" covers laws from the current
session back through 1996.

b. Massachusetts Code

Lexis Advance and Westlaw include full-text, searchable sources of their
Massachusetts annotated codes. The Lexis Advance source is called "Annotated
Laws of Massachusetts." The Westlaw source is "Massachusetts Statutes and
Court Rules."[13] These sources collate changes to code sections on a continuous
basis.[14] Bloomberg Law's version of the Massachusetts code currently has limited
annotations because its code annotations are under development.

Sometimes a problem requires you to refer to a version of a statute that is
no longer in effect. Only Westlaw currently offers historical versions of its annotated code. The "Massachusetts Statutes Annotated–Historical" source contains annual versions of the annotated code for each year going back to 1987.

IV. Sources for Federal Statutes

A. Print Sources

1. Federal Session Laws

In print, the session laws enacted by the U.S. Congress are collected in the
United States Statutes at Large. This set includes every law enacted by Congress
in order of the date of its passage. In its print version, the *Statutes at Large*
is the official source for the laws and resolutions passed by Congress, for proposed and ratified amendments to the U.S. Constitution, and for presidential
proclamations. The *Statutes at Large* is published by the Government Publishing Office.

2. Federal Code

The official codification of general and permanent federal statutes is *United
States Code* (USC). Organized by subject, USC has fifty-four titles. Within
each title, individual statutes are assigned section numbers. To cite a federal
statute, include both the title and the section number. For example, the citation
to the federal statute granting appellate jurisdiction to federal appellate courts

---

13. Westlaw also has a source with an unofficial, unannotated code, called "Massachusetts Statutes — Unannotated."

14. You may still need to take an additional step to update a code section fully. See
Part V.C. below on updating statutes.

is 28 U.S.C. § 1291 (2012). Title 28 is devoted to courts and judicial matters; 1291 is the section number assigned to this statute. The date of publication of that volume of USC was 2012.

USC is updated infrequently and does not include annotations, so it is of limited value in research. The more commonly used print sources are *United States Code Annotated* (USCA), published by West, and *United States Code Service* (USCS), published by LexisNexis. If the current text of a statute is not yet available in USC, citing USCA or USCS is preferred over citing an online source. Even if you use Lexis Advance, Westlaw, Bloomberg Law, or another online source to find a federal statute, cite to the official code unless the statute has been too recently amended for the current text to appear in the current official code. In that situation, cite to an unofficial print code.

Both the USCA and the USCS sets contain the text of federal statutes and references to related research sources. Both USCA and USCS include annotations called "Notes of Decisions" and "Case Notes," respectively, that refer to cases interpreting or applying each federal statute. USCA and USCS are updated through pocket parts and paperback supplements. When only portions of a statute have changed, the pocket part may refer to the unchanged language in the hardbound volume. Other pocket parts are cumulative, so a modified statute will be reprinted in full.

Both annotated code publications contain information other than the text of statutes and case annotations. For example, they provide references to federal regulations and executive orders and to secondary sources. Both USCA and USCS include helpful tables, including tables listing statutes by their popular names. Both also contain federal court rules.

B. Online Sources

Federal statutes and a wealth of federal legislative materials are available for free online and through commercial research services.

1. Session Laws and Other Legislative Materials

The official compilation of federal session laws is *Statutes at Large*. The Government Publishing Office's Federal Digital System ("FDsys") is a free internet resource providing access to the *Statutes at Large*. FDsys is scheduled to be replaced in 2017 with govinfo.gov, which was in beta testing as this book was being finalized. Both FDsys and the govinfo.gov beta site provide *Statutes at Large* coverage back to 1951. Subscription services, such as Lexis Advance, Westlaw, and HeinOnline, provide coverage back to the 1700s.

FDsys lets users search and browse recent legislative materials, including the full text of bills back to 1993 and bill histories back to 1984. Congress.gov,[15] a website maintained by the Library of Congress, is another resource for searching and browsing legislative materials. Some of its sources go back to the 1970s; others have more limited coverage. Lexis Advance, Westlaw, and Bloomberg Law also include relatively recent legislative materials.

2. Federal Code

The body that codifies the U.S. Code, the Office of Law Revision Counsel of the House of Representatives, offers a searchable and browsable version on its website. FDsys also offers a searchable and browsable version of the code. The Office of Law Revision Counsel and FDsys provide access to current and historical versions of the federal code back to 1994. These versions of the code are unannotated.

Commercial research services for the federal code include Lexis Advance, Westlaw, Bloomberg Law, and VersusLaw. Lexis Advance, Westlaw, and Bloomberg Law have annotated federal code sources. Lexis Advance and Westlaw also provide archived federal statutes dating to the early 1990s. Lexis Advance, Westlaw and Bloomberg Law offer searchable popular name tables and browsable tables of contents for their federal code sources. In addition, Westlaw has a searchable general index for its annotated federal code. Other commercial research services such as Fastcase and VersusLaw provide more limited coverage at a generally lower price than the leading commercial research services

V. Working with Massachusetts Statutes

Researching a problem that is controlled by statutory authority requires several steps. You must identify relevant statutes; make sure you have the text of the statutes that are currently in effect (or the text that was in effect at the point in time relevant to your client's problem); read and understand the relevant statutes; and read cases or other materials that interpret, apply, or analyze the statutes.[16]

---

15. Congress.gov replaces THOMAS, a comprehensive online research platform launched in the mid-1990s. As of this printing, THOMAS is still active, but the Library of Congress expects to retire THOMAS within a few years. The website for THOMAS is http://thomas.loc.gov/home/thomas.php.

16. This material may include administrative regulations, which are covered in Chapter 8.

Although these steps are listed above in sequence, in any given research project you may decide to take some of them out of order. For example, if a secondary source identifies a leading case that interprets a section of the statute, you may decide to read the case before reading all the cross-referenced sections.

You may also decide to use a combination of print and electronic resources, perhaps using print sources to find an entry point and to skim potentially relevant statutes, and using electronic sources to update relevant statutes. Table 6-1 outlines a general process for researching in the Massachusetts code in print or online.

Table 6-1. Overview: Researching *Massachusetts General Laws*

Step #1	Obtain an entry point through a supervisor, secondary source, popular name table, index search, or natural-language search of an online source and locate potentially relevant statutory sections.
Step #2	Focus on relevant sections after skimming *potentially* relevant sections to identify those that are *probably* relevant, browsing the statute's table of contents to find related sections and skimming any cross-referenced sections to assess whether and how they apply to your problem.
Step #3	Update each relevant section of the statute to make sure you are reading the version that is currently in effect.
Step #4	Carefully read each relevant section of the statute to understand what it says.
Step #5	Use the annotations to each relevant section to find citations to binding primary authorities (regulations or cases) that interpret or apply the section, and analyze these authorities.
Step #6	As appropriate, use the annotations to find citations to secondary sources that analyze each section.

A. Enter the Code to Locate Potentially Relevant Sections

1. Entry by Citation

If you have the citation to an applicable statute, you can use the citation to locate the statute in print or online. To use a citation to enter MGLA or ALM in print, skim the spines of the set, locate the volume that contains the chapter and section you were given, and open the volume to the proper page. For example, if the question you are researching is whether a breach of contract to marry is actionable, and your supervisor cites you to Mass. Gen. Laws ch. 207, § 47A, you could peruse the spines of the volumes of the MGLA or ALM set until you come to the volume that includes chapter 207, and then open the volume to the appropriate chapter and section.

To locate a statute by citation on Lexis Advance, Westlaw, or Bloomberg Law, you can either type the citation in the search box or browse for the chapter and section in the table of contents. Consult each service for its specific citation format.

2. Entry by Popular Name

You can also use a popular name table as an entry point. For example, if you know that the problem involves the Consumer Protection Act, you could look that up in a popular name table in print or online. In print, peruse the spines of the volumes toward the end of the code set to find the popular name table. Browse until you find the popular name of the act and the reference to Chapter 93A of the Massachusetts General Laws. Then, locate the statute by skimming the spines of the print MGLA or ALM set.

You can also find popular name tables online. To use the popular name table in Westlaw, choose the "Massachusetts statutes index" source and either search or browse for "Consumer Protection," which will link to Chapter 93A.[17] The Massachusetts Trial Court Law Libraries have also compiled a popular name table that links to statutes as well as regulations and, in some cases, other authorities.[18] This table is less comprehensive than the tables in the official or annotated print codes or Westlaw's online table.

3. Entry Through a Table of Contents

In some circumstances, you may want to enter the code through a table of contents. Each ALM volume begins with a general table of contents identifying the titles of the code, and each ALM title and chapter begins with a more detailed table of contents. MGLA also includes detailed tables of contents at the beginning of each title and chapter, but includes a general table of contents only in Volume 1. You can also browse or search the tables of contents to the annotated codes on Lexis Advance, Westlaw, and Bloomberg Law.

---

17. Lexis Advance and Bloomberg Law do not offer popular name tables for Massachusetts statutes.

18. The Massachusetts Trial Court Law Libraries offer a variety of references on their website, http://www.mass.gov/courts/case-legal-res/law-lib/.

4. Entry Through an Index

To enter the code by means of the index, first generate a list of search terms by reflecting on the issue or using a set of standard questions.[19] If you are working in print with the ALM or MGLA, pull the appropriate index volume and look up your search terms. Do not stop reviewing the index when you find one reference to a statute because several statutes may address your issue. Also, remember that indexes are layered. One search term may lead to another search term, which in turn may lead to a relevant statute.

You can also access indexes online. Westlaw's "Massachusetts Statutes Index" is an online version of the MGLA print index. The Massachusetts Trial Court Law Libraries also offer two indexes to help you find statutes as well as other authorities and research guides. First, the resource "Massachusetts Laws About ..." offers a browsable index by subject. Second, the resource "Massachusetts Laws by Popular Name" contains not only popular names but also subject entries that you would find in a traditional index. Both of these resources are less comprehensive than the indexes in the official or annotated print codes or in Westlaw's online index.

5. Entry Through Full-Text Search

You may also find an entry point by running a natural-language search on Lexis Advance or Westlaw. Because full-text searching requires you to predict statutory language, full-text searching may not be as effective as using an index. Avoid using terms-and-connectors searching to locate a statute initially because this type of search requires you to predict statutory language and syntax with great precision.

Consider this example of full-text searching. You represent a church that wants to expand its building but is concerned about zoning restrictions. You might use the following natural-language search in Lexis Advance's "Annotated Laws of Massachusetts" source: "religious zoning exemption." Although that natural-language search would turn up hundreds of statutes that are not relevant to your problem, the first item on the result list is Mass. Gen. Laws ch. 40A, § 3. Clicking on that citation takes you to the text of the statute, which provides, in relevant part, "No zoning ordinance or by-law shall ... regulate or restrict the use of land or structures for religious purposes ... [,] provided, however, that such land or structures may be subject to reasonable regulations concerning the bulk and height of structures and determining yard sizes, lot

---

19. Chapter 2 describes ways to generate a list of search terms.

area, setbacks, open space, parking and building coverage requirements."
Crafting a terms-and-connectors search to locate this language may be chal-
lenging.

B. Focus on Relevant Sections

An entry point may lead to a result list of several potentially relevant statutes.
At this point in your research, keep your mind open. Before deciding that a
single statute is the key to your problem, consider all of the statutes on your
result list. While one statute may seem right on point, the legislature may have
enacted a more general or more specific statute that applies to your problem.
For example, Mass. Gen. Laws ch. 90, § 70N, allows a purchaser of a motor
vehicle to void the sale in certain circumstances. Mass. Gen. Laws ch. 93A,
§ 9, allows a consumer to sue for treble damages for unfair or deceptive trade
practices. Stopping your research upon finding only one of these statutes might
result in an incomplete picture of the remedies available to your client.

To avoid committing to a single statute too early, skim the group of *potentially* relevant statutes to identify those that are *probably* relevant. Only after
skimming the text of a number of these statutes will you be in a position to
focus on the section or group of sections that is most relevant to your problem.
As part of your assessment of which sections are *probably* relevant, you may
decide to look at case annotations interpreting or applying sections you are
considering.[20] Reading the summaries of these cases may help you determine
whether a statute applies to the type of problem you are researching. Following
up on cross-references to regulations may also help you figure out whether
you are in the right place in the code.

Codes generally group related provisions together, so after you decide that
a section is probably relevant, go to the table of contents to survey the "neigh-
borhood" of your code section. This step may help you find a section defining
terms in your code section or other related provisions. For example, before
entering plea bargaining negotiations with a prosecutor, a lawyer whose client
has been charged with burglary under Mass. Gen. Laws ch. 266, § 14, would
want to be aware of other related offenses that carry lesser penalties.

At this point in your research, you may decide to look at statutes (if any)
that are cross-referenced within your statute; this task may help you confirm
your tentative decision that the statute you are working with is relevant. Or

---

20. In both print and online versions of annotated codes, case annotations are included after other research aids that follow the text of the statute.

you may find it is more useful to wait to follow up on cross-references until the point at which you are ready to read and analyze carefully the language of the principal statute with which you are working.

C. Update Relevant Sections

Once you have determined that a statute is probably relevant to your problem, you must update it to make sure that you have the version that is currently in effect.[21] The legislature might amend or repeal a statute, and that legislative action may not be reflected in the source in which you first read the statute. The process of updating a federal statute is similar to the process of updating a Massachusetts statute, although of course the specific sources differ.

1. Updating in Print

Ordinarily, you must take several steps to fully update a statute in a print code. Because print updates cover specific time periods, you may have to piece together successive updates to get a complete picture.

A print volume in an MGLA or ALM set may be updated with several successive cumulative annual pocket parts before the publisher decides to issue a new volume that integrates the latest pocket part with the text in the main volume. At some point, the pocket part may be too thick to fit in the pocket at the back of the volume. In this situation, the publisher may issue a free-standing supplement before issuing a new volume.

To begin updating a statute in print, look for a pocket part in the volume you are using.[22] In the pocket part, look up the section you are working with and note any changes to the statute. If there are new case annotations, note them so you can look them up later without having to come back to the pocket part. Go through the same process with any interim updating pamphlets. Then, on the front cover of the last updating pamphlet note the date or legislative session with which the update "closed."

---

21. Sometimes the relevant version of the statute is no longer in effect. For example, if you are trying to determine whether your client is entitled to a refund of taxes paid during a prior tax year, you would ordinarily need to look at the version of the statute that was in effect then, not at the version that is in effect at the present time. In this situation, consult a historical code source, as described above in Part III.B.2.b.

22. If the volume was published before the current year and has no pocket part, the pocket part may have been too thick to insert in the pocket in the volume; in this situation, look on the shelf for a free-standing supplement or ask a librarian.

Consult advance legislative service pamphlets for later legislation affecting the section. To do this, use the table in the pamphlet that correlates session laws with the code sections they affect. When using a legislative service, always note whether the pamphlets it issues are supplemental, in which case you must check every pamphlet, or cumulative, in which case you must check only the most recent pamphlet.

Because of the realities of printing and distribution, you cannot be sure you have fully updated a statute even after having consulted the most recent print update. At that point, you can update the statute more fully by checking recent session laws, either on the website of the Massachusetts legislature[23] or through Lexis Advance, Westlaw, or Bloomberg Law.

2. Updating Online

Even researchers who do most of their work in print also use Lexis Advance, Westlaw, or Bloomberg Law to update statutes because the electronic updating process is more streamlined and is generally more precise. On each commercial research service, when you retrieve a section of the code, you will see a "Currentness" description that indicates the most recent session laws included in the version of the code you are viewing. Even if recently enacted session law changes have not yet been incorporated into the commercial research service's current version of the code, you will see a citator signal or flag indicating enacted or pending legislation.

If you are using free internet resources, you will need to update your section of the code manually. The General Court's online version of the Massachusetts General Laws indicates the most recent session laws that are included online. To update a given code section, you must review the online session laws to determine whether any recently-enacted session laws affect your code section.

3. Updating with a Citator

On Lexis Advance and Westlaw, you may update a statute using each service's citator. The citator shows any enacted or proposed legislation that would affect the statute. Bloomberg Law's citator, BCite, currently does not apply to statutes.

---

23. The website is www.malegislature.gov.

D. Carefully Read the Statute to Understand What It Says

Statutes require very close reading because they are drafted extremely densely. Read slowly because every word in a statute is significant. Pay careful attention to syntax, especially to conjunctions like "and" and "or." To be sure you understand the relationships among a statute's clauses, phrases, and words, consider outlining the statute or creating a flow chart. Be attuned to the possibility that syntax may be ambiguous: sentence structure may not make clear what word or phrase a modifier modifies.

As you read, identify specific terms that are vague or ambiguous. If a term is vague or ambiguous, check to see if it has a statutory definition. If there is no statutory definition, use the annotations to see if the term has been interpreted by a court or by an administrative agency charged with implementing the statute.

If your statute has been amended, be sure that the version you are reading integrates amendments with the previous text of the statute. Also, at this point review statutes that are cross-referenced within the text of your statute because these statutes are incorporated by reference into the text of your statute.

After reading a statute carefully, you may decide that the statute does not apply to your problem after all. In that situation, go back to the drawing board to identify *possibly* relevant primary authority.

E. Use Annotations to Locate Primary Sources That Interpret or Apply the Statute

Sometimes, it is clear from the text of a statute how it applies to your problem. In most situations, however, you must look at other primary authority in conjunction with the statute. Annotated codes provide entry points for research into that primary authority through references to related administrative regulations and through summaries of cases that interpret or apply a given statute.

Do not rely on the references in an annotated code to be comprehensive. Rather, treat these references as entry points, and expand and validate your research using the full panoply of sources and techniques that are available to you.[24]

Summaries of cases interpreting or applying a statute are another valuable feature following the text of a statute in a print or electronic annotated code.

---

24. Chapter 2 provides an overview of the research process.

When there are many relevant cases, an annotated code organizes them topically in sections and provides an outline to the sections in advance of the first summary. Note that the case citations in these summaries are not necessarily in correct citation form. Figure 6-3 shows the outline and the first several summaries of cases interpreting or applying Mass. Gen. Laws ch. 210, §7, which addresses the rights of an adopted child to succeed to property of the adopting parent.[25]

F. Use References to Secondary Sources If Appropriate

For some legal problems, secondary sources are useful primarily for background and as finding tools. For others, secondary sources may be useful as persuasive authority. Annotated codes provide references to related secondary sources as well as to related primary sources. Each major commercial publisher favors its own publications, but also cites to law reviews and other legal periodicals. In addition to references to secondary sources, MGLA includes references to topics and key numbers in the West Key Number System.

VI. Working with Statutes of Other States

The process of working with statutes of other states is similar to the process of working with Massachusetts statutes, but you will encounter differences. State classification systems for statutes differ widely. For example, California and New York classify their statutes by topic rather than by chapter. Thus, the California statute invalidating certain covenants not to compete is California Business and Professional Code § 16600. Oregon gives its statutes a single number: for example, Oregon Revised Statutes § 164.225 is the first-degree burglary statute.

State codes are widely available online. Free internet resources, such as the Cornell Legal Information Institute,[26] provide gateways to state statutory materials. Lexis Advance, Westlaw, and Bloomberg Law provide annotated versions of state codes and bill-tracking information, although Bloomberg Law's annotations are under development and are less comprehensive than the other commercial research services' annotations.

---

25. See also Figure 2-1, which shows case summaries interpreting or applying Mass. Gen. Laws ch. 93A, §9, in the *Annotated Laws of Massachusetts* on Lexis Advance.

26. This site is accessible through www.law.cornell.edu.

Figure 6-3. Case Annotations

210 § 7 ADOPTION; CHANGE OF NAMES

Adoption and Safe Families Act, child welfare system. Jim Moye & Roberta Rinker, 39 Harv. J. on Legis. 375 (No.2, Summer 2002).

Adoption nunc pro tunc. Emil Slizewski, 16 Ann.Surv.Mass.L. 124 (1969).

Collateral inheritance by adopted children. 38 Harv.L.Rev. 976 (1925).

Family relations and persons. Banks McDowell, 12 Ann.Surv.Mass.L. 86 (1965).

Law governing moveables under will. Francis J. Nicholson, 11 Ann.Surv.Mass.L. 87 (1964).

Status of "recognized" children, right to inherit. Monroe Inker, 3 Ann.Surv.Mass.L. 87, 88 (1956).

Library References

Adoption ☞18 to 24.
Westlaw Topic No. 17.

C.J.S. Adoption of Persons §§ 136 to 138, 140 to 150, 152 to 154, 156 to 164.

Research References

Treatises and Practice Aids

3 Mass. Prac. Series § 63:33, Succession to Property and the Adopted Child.
21 Mass. Prac. Series § 22.5, Petition for Probate of Will.
21 Mass. Prac. Series § 30.6, Identification of Legatee.
21 Mass. Prac. Series § 8.11, Rights of Adopted Children.
23 Mass. Prac. Series § 11.23, Definitions.

28 Mass. Prac. Series § 16.8, Intestacy -- Descent and Distribution.
5B Mass. Prac. Series § 31:27, Provisions for Children.
5B Mass. Prac. Series § 31:85, Construction of Wills.
14A Mass. Prac. Series § 8.135, Post-Adoption Issues -- Inheritance Rights.
14C Mass. Prac. Series § 22.121, Distribution -- Intestate.

Notes of Decisions

Adoption in another state 13
Construction and application 2
Decree of adoption 7
Heirs of adopted child 11
Inheritance from natural parent 4
Issue or heir of adopting parent 5
Kindred of adopting parent 9
Kindred of natural parent 8
Legal descendants of adopting parent 10
Omission from will 6
Retroactive effect 3
Rights of siblings of adopted child 12
Validity of prior laws 1

---

1. Validity of prior laws

G.S.1860, c. 110, § 7, which substantially re-enacted St.1871, c. 310, making an adopted child legally the child of the parents by adoption, was not unconstitutional, unless it interfered with vested rights. Sewall v. Roberts (1874) 115 Mass. 262.

2. Construction and application

Application of 1967 statutory amendment precluding adopted child from inheriting property of his intestate natural kindred to persons adopted both before and after effective date of amendment raises no significant constitutional

question; adopted child's possibility of inheritance from his natural kindred is not interest of such substance as to be entitled to constitutional protection, particularly where adopted child has in substitution a new set of expectancies. Katz v. Koronchik (1975) 338 N.E.2d 339, 369 Mass. 125. Constitutional Law ☞ 2634

In the case of Cobb v. Old Colony Trust Co. (1936) 3 N.E.2d 797, 295 Mass. 338, the court said: "The provisions of G.L.(Ter.Ed.) c. 210, § 7, relate exclusively to the rights of persons 'adopted in accordance with this chapter.' Those words, in the connection in which they stand, show that the General Court 'had solely in view adoption by or of inhabitants of this Commonwealth, and did not intend either to regulate the manner, or to define the effects, of adoption by and of inhabitants of other States according to the law of their domicil.' Ross v. Ross, 129 Mass. 243, 267, 37 Am.Rep. 321. Manifestly this section has no bearing upon the questions here to be decided because the adoption was decreed in Maine where all the parties were then inhabitants. The provisions of said section 7 refer to adoptions within and in conformity to the laws of this Commonwealth."

In the case of Boutlier v. City of Malden (1917) 116 N.E. 251, 226 Mass. 479, the court said: "this court has held that the intent of these sections of the statute (sections 6 and 7)

922

outline of case summaries

case summaries, arranged according to the outline

Source: *Massachusetts General Laws Annotated*, Vol. 33. Reprinted with permission of Thomson Reuters.

Chapter 7

Legislative Process and Legislative History

I. Introduction

This chapter gives an overview of the Massachusetts legislative process and researching both Massachusetts and federal legislative history.[1] A bill pending in the legislature may become a statute that affects your client's interests. To track a bill's path through the legislature, you must understand the legislative process.

Legislative history may help you interpret a statute that is vague or ambiguous or help you develop an argument for a particular reading of a statute. Legislative history includes the steps a bill took to become a statute as well as changes the legislature made to the statute after it was originally enacted. This material may yield information about the legislature's intent in enacting or amending the statute. Most Massachusetts legislation is not accompanied by a statement of purpose, and most legislative committees do not issue reports explaining their work. Thus, you will rarely find *direct* evidence of legislative

---

1. This chapter draws heavily on the following sources: Chapter 3 of *Handbook of Legal Research in Massachusetts* (Mary Ann Neary & Ruth Matz eds., 3d ed., Mass. CLE 2009 & Supps. 2012 & 2015); the website of the General Court at https://malegislature.gov. *Legal and Legislative Resources: Massachusetts Legislative History*, a summary of how to trace state legislative history, which is available on the state's website at www.mass.gov/anf/research-and-tech/legal-and-legislative-resources/tracing-ma-law.htm; and *Massachusetts Legislative History*, a comprehensive discussion of the state legislative process available on the State Library of Massachusetts (the "State Library") website at http://archives.lib.state.ma.us/handle/2452/35648. See these sources for more detailed information on the topics discussed in this chapter.

intent.[2] Massachusetts courts do, however, *infer* intent from legislative action.[3] Thus, when you work with a statute, consider the possibility that legislative history research will yield useful information.

II. Massachusetts Legislative Process

A. The Massachusetts Legislature

The official name of the Massachusetts legislature is the "General Court." This name reflects the judicial powers the legislature had in colonial times. The General Court has two houses: the Senate, with 40 members, and the House of Representatives, with 160 members. The General Court meets in two-year terms called "sessions." Each session begins in an odd-numbered year.

B. How Legislation Is Enacted

The legislative process in Massachusetts is similar in general to the legislative process in the U.S. Congress and in the legislatures of other states, but differs in specifics. The Massachusetts House and Senate have separate rules to govern the progress of a bill through each legislative branch, and there is a third set of joint rules.[4]

The legislative process begins when an idea becomes a proposal for legislation. In Massachusetts, there are several ways in which a proposal for legislation may begin the process of becoming a law. In most situations, the process begins when a legislator files a petition, accompanied by a bill or resolve[5] setting forth

---

2. Some Massachusetts acts have a preamble that indicates legislative intent. Legislation proposed by the Governor, a state officer, an administrative agency, or a special commission may be accompanied by material indicating the purpose of the proposed legislation.

3. *See 81 Spooner Road LLC v. Town of Brookline*, 452 Mass. 109, 115 (2008). There, the Supreme Judicial Court adopted the reasoning in an unreported opinion of the Land Court, where the judge inferred legislative intent from the legislature's addition of an anti-snob zoning clause in the Massachusetts Zoning Enabling Act after the New Jersey Supreme Court upheld a by-law imposing a minimum floor area for single-family homes. *Id.* at 115–17.

4. The text of these rules is available through a link from the website of the General Court, https://malegislature.gov.

5. A "resolve" differs from an "act" because a resolve, unlike an act, is temporary in nature. Bills become acts when they are enacted by the legislature; a resolve remains a resolve throughout the process. *See* Louis Adam Frothingham, *A Brief History of the Constitution and Government of Massachusetts* 118 (Harvard U. 1916). An example of

the text of the proposed law, in the Office of the House or Senate Clerk. The process may also begin when the Governor recommends legislation in a "Governor's message," when a state administrative agency makes departmental recommendation, when a special commission or special committee submits a report recommending legislation, or when a joint standing committee of the House and Senate files a "committee bill." Legislation may also originate by voter initiative.[6]

While an idea for legislation may originate with a member of the House or the Senate or with a staff member, an idea for legislation may also originate with an individual, a business, or a non-profit group. In that situation, a lawyer who works outside government may be involved in drafting proposed legislation.[7] The proponent of legislation that originates outside the legislature must find a legislative sponsor to endorse the legislation.[8]

After a bill is filed in the Office of the House or Senate Clerk, it receives a bill number and is referred to the appropriate joint committee of the House and Senate, which then holds a public hearing. The *Bulletin of Committee Work* records the work of legislative committees during a legislative session. It is published on an ongoing basis and is available from the Legislative Document Room at the State House. It is not available online.[9]

---

a resolve filed in the House during the 2009–2010 legislative session is H.B. 3420, providing for an investigation and study by a special commission relative to adolescents at risk. That resolve was referred to the Joint Committee on Children and Families; no further action was taken.

6. *See* Mass. Const. amend. art. 48 (providing for legislation by voter initiative and for voter referendum on already enacted legislation). The multi-stage process through which legislation that originates by voter initiative may become law is summarized at the website of the Office of the Attorney General at www.mass.gov/ago/government-resources/initiatives-and-other-ballot-questions/initiative-petition-process.html. An amendment to the Commonwealth's constitution may also be proposed by voter initiative. For a detailed review of resources on initiatives and referendums, see Spencer E. Clough, *Democracy's Harvest*, 26 Legal Ref. Serv. Q. 113 (2007).

7. The House and Senate Counsel have issued a *Legislative Research and Drafting Manual* to assist legislative lawyers and others who draft bills. This manual is available at https://malegislature.gov/legislation/draftingmanual.

8. A citizen may file a petition without sponsorship by a legislator, but a member must endorse it for presentation. *See Massachusetts Legislative History, supra* note 1, § 1.2.1.

9. Cumulative annual *Bulletins* are available in some law libraries, including the State Library. The website of the General Court, https://malegislature.gov, provides links to information about committee work during the current legislative session.

A bill must have three "readings" to become law. When the bill is reported by the joint committee, the first reading is publication in the *Journal* of the House or the Senate, depending on the chamber in which the bill originated.[10] The bill is then placed on the calendar of that chamber for its second reading, at which time it is open to debate and amendment.[11] The text of proposed amendments and procedural motions are recorded in the House or Senate *Journal*. After the members of the chamber have opportunity to debate the bill, the members vote on whether to refer the bill for a third reading. If there is favorable action on the bill following the third reading, the bill is "passed to be engrossed." Then, the bill is sent to the Engrossing Division of the General Court, which prints the text of the bill to be considered by the other chamber.

The second chamber considers the bill according to the procedure outlined above. If the bill is not amended by the second chamber, it goes to the Engrossing Division, which prepares the final text of the bill and returns it to each chamber for formal enactment. Then, the Senate President transmits the bill to the Governor for approval.

When the two chambers cannot agree on the same text of a bill, the bill goes to a Conference Committee, which issues as its report a new draft of the bill. This new draft may have a new bill number. The new draft cannot be amended. If both chambers accept the new draft, it is enacted and the Senate President transmits the bill to the Governor.

Within the following ten days, the Governor must sign the bill, return it with amendment, or veto it. Otherwise, the bill becomes law without the Governor's signature. If, however, the legislative session ends within the ten-day period, a bill that is not signed by the Governor does not become law.

---

10. The House or Senate *Journal* is the record of the daily business of the respective chamber. It does not include debates. House *Journals* from January 24, 2001 to present are available on the website of the General Court at https://malegislature.gov/People/ClerksOffice/House/Journal. Senate *Journals* from March 12, 1998 to present are available at https://malegislature.gov/People/ClerksOffice/Senate/Journal. Westlaw's "Massachusetts Legislative History: Journals" source has House *Journals* going back to 2001, Senate *Journals* going back to 1998, and Joint Session *Journals* going back to 2000. Lexis Advance does not have the full text of Massachusetts legislative *Journals*.

11. Although there is no official transcript of legislative debate, formal sessions are broadcast on public television, and video recordings of these broadcasts are deposited in the State Library. Live and archived webcasts of formal sessions of the House and Senate are also available at www.masslegislature.tv. State House News Service, a commercial service, makes available to its subscribers unofficial records of, and reporting on, legislative proceedings, including transcripts of some debates. The website is www.statehousenews.com. The State Library subscribes to print files of this service.

General laws become effective ninety days after being signed by the Governor. Acts that are accompanied by an emergency preamble, which must be adopted by both chambers, become effective when the Governor signs the legislation. Special acts take effect thirty days after signing, unless the act provides otherwise. Resolves take effect immediately.

III. Tracking Current Massachusetts Legislation

If a bill has been introduced that may affect your client's interests, you can track the bill's progress through the legislature. You will probably use online tools for this task, although it is possible to track a bill in print using the *Bulletin of Committee Work* and House and Senate *Journals*.

The text of bills filed in the current and recent session of the House and Senate is available on the General Court website. If you have the bill number, use the General Court's Bills Search page[12] to retrieve the bill in either PDF or HTML format. If you do not have the bill number, use the search box to search for a bill with a relevant word or phrase.

After you read the text of the bill, the next step is to look at the "bill history" to see what, if anything, has happened to the bill. The bill history is an abstract of the bill and information about its path through the legislature. Figure 7-1 shows the bill history of Senate Bill No. 1987 of the 186th Session of the General Court (2009–2010).

Lexis Advance has separate sources for the full text of bills, "MA Full-Text Bills," and for bill tracking reports, "MA Bill Tracking Reports." Full-text bills are available from 1991 through the current legislative session. Bill histories are available from 1989 through the current session. If you have the bill number, type it in the search box. If you pull up a bill, you can retrieve the bill tracking report by clicking on a link within the document. Similarly, if you pull up a bill tracking report, you can retrieve the corresponding bill by clicking on a link within the document. Both sources are searchable by natural language or terms and connectors.

Westlaw has several sources from which you can retrieve the text of a bill introduced during the current legislative session or track the process of the bill through the current session. The "Massachusetts Proposed Legislation" source contains bills introduced in the current session. "Massachusetts Bill Tracking" contains bill tracking information as well as links to the full text of bills introduced in the current session. As with Lexis Advance, if you pull up

---

12. The website is https://malegislature.gov/Bills/Search.

Figure 7-1. Bill History

Bill S.1987

An Act relative to first aid kits and fire extinguishers on trains.

For legislation relative to first aid kits and fire extinguishers on trains

Sponsors: Steven A. Tolman

Status:

Download text: View Formatted Document   Download PDF

186th (2009 - 2010)

Print Preview

| Current Bill Text | Bill History |

Actions for Bill S.1987

Date	Branch	Action
1/20/2009	Senate	Referred to the committee on Transportation
1/20/2009	House	House concurred
2/4/2010	Senate	Bill reported favorably by committee and referred to the committee on Senate Ways and Means
1/4/2011	Senate	No further action taken

a bill, you can retrieve the bill tracking report by clicking a link within the document. Similarly, if you pull up a bill tracking report, you can retrieve the corresponding bill by clicking a link within the document. Both sources are searchable by natural language or terms and connectors.

Instatrac, a commercial legislative tracking service, allows subscribers to search the texts of bills and bill histories for the current legislative session and for sessions going back to 1995–1996. The State Library offers on-site access to Instatrac.

Bloomberg Law currently contains no resources for Massachusetts bills or legislative history.

IV. Compiling a Massachusetts Legislative History

Compiling a legislative history is the converse of tracking a bill. To track a bill, you move forward through time as a bill progresses through the legislature. To compile a legislative history, you move backward through time from a statute that has already been enacted.

While the legislative history of a statute may shed light on its meaning, far less legislative history material is available for Massachusetts statutes than is available for federal statutes. Most legislation in Massachusetts is filed by petition and, unlike federal legislation, is not accompanied by a statement explaining its purpose.[13] Unlike congressional committees, committees of the Massachusetts legislature do not produce narrative reports; rather, they make their recommendations to the members of the respective chambers on a standard form.[14] Moreover, there are no official transcripts of legislative debates or committee hearings.[15]

---

13. If legislation is proposed by the Governor, a state agency, or special commission, it will ordinarily be accompanied by material explaining the purpose of the proposed legislation.

14. In rare cases, the legislative documents will include reports prepared by the now-defunct Massachusetts Legislative Research Council. Selected reports are available online through the New England Law | Boston library at http://www.nesl.edu/research/Legislative_Council.cfm.

15. Streaming and archived videos of sessions beginning in 2006 are available at www.masslegislature.tv, and video recordings of debates from legislative sessions beginning in the 1980s are archived at the State Library. Unofficial reports on and coverage of debates are available to subscribers of State House News Service, a commercial service, at www.statehousenews.com. State House News Service is available free to members of the Social Law Library, either in-library or online through the Social Law Library website. See Chapter 8, note 18, for a description of the Social Law Library.

You may be able to glean some information about legislative intent from documents in the "legislative package," which contains the proposal for legislation as originally filed and other official documents filed as the bill progressed through the legislature. It may also include other materials, such as letters concerning the bill. Legislative packages, as well as legislative files from the Office of the Governor, are held in the Massachusetts Archives, commonly referred to as the State Archives.[16] Table 7-1 summarizes the steps involved in compiling a Massachusetts legislative history.[17]

Table 7-1. Compiling a Massachusetts Legislative History*

1. Select the law to trace, whether it is a statute as originally enacted or an amendment that changed a statute in a way that is relevant to your client's problem.

2. Find the final bill number of the statute.
   - Use the "credits" following the text of the statute in an annotated code to locate the session law number of the statute and of any amendments.
   - Use the session law number to find the bill number in other sources.
     - For laws enacted since 1997, use the session laws files on the General Court website, which include final bill numbers.
     - In print, use the table at the end of each annual *Bulletin of Committee Work* that provides the final bill number for each session law enacted during the year.
     - On Lexis Advance, use the "Massachusetts Advance Legislative Service" source to retrieve a session law enacted in 1990 or after, along with its final bill number. Type the citation to the session law in the search box. A link from the session law will lead you to a bill tracking statement, which shows the path of the bill through the legislature.
     - On Westlaw, use the "Massachusetts Historical Session Laws" source to retrieve session laws enacted from 1987 through the legislative session preceding the current session. Type the citation to the session law in the search box. A link from the session law will show the final bill number, and will link to drafts of bills and entries in the House or Senate *Journals*.**

---

16. The State Archives contain state government records dating back to 1629 as well as a variety of private collections. For an overview of the Massachusetts Archives' holdings, see http://www.sec.state.ma.us/arc/arcidx.htm.

17. For a detailed guide to the process of tracing the legislative history of a Massachusetts statute, see *Handbook of Legal Research in Massachusetts, supra* note 1, at § 3.10 or *Massachusetts Legislative History, supra* note 1.

Table 7-1. Compiling a Massachusetts Legislative History, *continued*

3. Use the final bill number to obtain a complete bill history.
    *   Bill histories from the past three legislative sessions, as well as the current session, can be obtained through links from the website of the General Court.
    *   For legislation enacted from 2006 onward, Lexis Advance's "Massachusetts Legislative Bill History" source allows you to retrieve the session law with a link to a bill tracking statement. Limited coverage is available for legislation enacted from 2002 to 2005.
    *   Westlaw's "Massachusetts Advance Legislative Service" source yields information for legislation enacted in 1987 and after.
    *   For legislation enacted in 1970 and after, use the Bill History Index in the last volume of the House or Senate *Journal* for the year the statute was enacted.
    *   For older legislation, a bill history must be compiled from several sources, so it is advisable to consult a librarian.

4. Use the bill history to lead you to prior versions of the bill and amendments.

5. Examine the legislative package in the State Archives for the original version of the bill and any notes or letters that may shed light on legislative intent. Also examine any special commission reports.

---

* Sources for this table are the authorities listed in note 1, *supra*, the website of the General Court, Lexis Advance, and Westlaw.

** The "Massachusetts Enacted Legislation (Session Laws)" source has session laws enacted during the current session, and also provides links to drafts of bills and *Journal* entries.

Important sources for related official and unofficial documents that may shed light on the statute are in the State Library and the State Archives.[18] The collection of the State Library includes video recordings of some House and Senate sessions and selected committee hearings, indexes to special reports authorized by the General Court, Governor's messages, and selected late 18th- and early 19th-century Massachusetts newspapers as well as legislative documents dating back to colonial times. The holdings of the State Archives include the legislative package for each bill from 1629 to present, unenacted legislation, House and Senate dockets, roll calls, *Journals*, and committee and legislative commission hearing files. The State Archives also has legislative files prepared by the Office of the Governor. Materials available from State

---

18. For descriptions of the major sources of documentation for legislative action, see *Handbook of Legal Research in Massachusetts, supra* note 1, at § 3.10.2.

House News Service[19] or on Instatrac,[20] including records of debates, may also be helpful.

To increase the probability of compiling an accurate and useful legislative history, seek the assistance of a librarian. Reference librarians at the State Library have particular expertise in this area.

V. Federal Legislation

In general, the federal legislative process produces more information about legislative intent. Sources of federal legislative history are relatively easy to locate in print or online.

A. Federal Bill Tracking

Government websites make available much information about legislative action during the current session. In general, you will access that information through the number of the bill you are tracking.[21] The Library of Congress site[22] provides bill summaries and status, committee reports, and the *Congressional Record* (which records debate in the House and Senate). The Government Publishing Office's Federal Digital System ("FDsys")[23] provides the text of bills, bill histories, selected hearings and reports, and the *Congressional Record*. FDsys is scheduled to be replaced in 2017 with govinfo.gov, which was in beta testing as this book was being finalized. Coverage of federal bill tracking varies even within a single site, so check carefully.

B. Federal Legislative History

Compiling the legislative history of a federal statute is likely to yield more useful information than compiling a Massachusetts legislative history. When a federal statute is enacted, it is published as a slip law and is assigned a "public law number." This number is in the form Pub. L. No. 110-233, where the numerals before the hyphen are the number of the Congress in which the law

---

19. See note 11 above for a description of this service.

20. See Part III of this chapter for a description of this service.

21. Federal bills are numbered sequentially in each chamber of Congress. Generally, Senate bill numbers are preceded by an "S," and House of Representatives bill numbers are preceded by "H.R."

22. The website is www.congress.gov.

23. The website is www.gpo.gov/fdsys.

was enacted and the numerals after the hyphen are assigned chronologically as bills are enacted. The public law number given above is for the *Genetic Information Nondiscrimination Act of 2008*, which was the 233rd law enacted during the 110th Congress.

The new statute is later published as a session law in *United States Statutes at Large*, which is the federal counterpart of the *Massachusetts Acts and Resolves*. Session laws are designated by volume and page in *Statutes at Large*, for example, 122 Stat. 881. Finally, the new statute is assigned a code citation when it is codified with statutes on similar topics in the United States Code. The portion of the *Genetic Information Nondiscrimination Act of 2008* that prohibits health insurers from establishing eligibility rules based on genetic information is codified at 42 U.S.C. § 300gg-53.

To begin federal legislative history research, you need the session law citation or public law number. For codified legislation, you can obtain this information by looking up the statute in an annotated code.

1. Sources of Federal Legislative History

When conducting federal legislative history research, you are looking primarily for committee reports, materials from committee hearings, and transcripts of floor debates. Committee reports are the most persuasive authority. Unlike reports of Massachusetts legislative committees, which are not narrative, congressional committee reports are often lengthy documents that contain the committee's analysis of the bill, the reasons for enacting it, and the views of any members who disagree with those reasons. Congressional hearing materials include transcripts from the proceedings as well as documents such as prepared testimony and exhibits.

Floor debates are published in the *Congressional Record*. Be wary in relying on these debates as they may not have actually been delivered in the House or Senate; members of Congress can amend their remarks and even submit written statements that are published in transcript form as if they were spoken. Table 7-2 compares sources for Massachusetts and federal legislative history.

Table 7-2. Comparison of Sources for Massachusetts and
Federal Legislative History

Action	Massachusetts Sources	Federal Sources
Committee work	These are short, standard form reports. No official transcripts of hearings are available. Video recordings and unofficial State House News Service reports of selected hearings may be available.	Reports written by committees are the most persuasive form of legislative history. Transcripts of hearings and other documents may also be available.
Debate	No official transcripts of debates exist. Video recordings and unofficial State House News Service reports of legislative sessions may be available.	*Congressional Record* publishes the statements of Senators and House members during debate.
Session law	*Massachusetts Acts and Resolves*	*United States Statutes at Large*
Codified version	*Massachusetts General Laws; Massachusetts General Laws Annotated; Annotated Laws of Massachusetts*	*United States Code; United States Code Annotated; United States Code Service*

2. Compiled Legislative History

Unlike in Massachusetts, there are compiled legislative histories of major federal statutes. A widely known reference book that compiles federal legislative histories is *Sources of Compiled Legislative Histories.*[24]

3. Print Sources for Federal Legislative History

Table 7-3 shows the most common print sources for researching federal legislative history. Some sources contain a "how to use" section at the beginning; otherwise, consult a reference librarian.

---

24. Nancy P. Johnson, *Sources of Compiled Legislative Histories: A Bibliography of Government Documents, Periodical Articles, and Books* (AALL 1979–present) (also available at www.heinonline.com).

Table 7-3. Selected Sources for Federal Legislative History in Print

Source	Contents
United States Code Congressional and Administrative News (USCCAN)	Selected reprints and excerpts of committee reports; references to other reports and to the *Congressional Record*
Congressional Information Service (CIS)	Full text of bills, committee reports, and hearings on microfiche; print indexes and abstracts in bound volumes
Congressional Record	Debate from the floor of the House and Senate

4. Online Sources for Federal Legislative History

The sites noted earlier in this chapter for tracking federal legislation also provide useful information for legislative history research. The Library of Congress site at www.congress.gov provides bill summaries, bill text, bill status, committee reports, and the *Congressional Record*. The Government Publishing Office's FDsys site (soon to be replace by govinfo.gov) contains bills, selected hearings and reports, as well as the *Congressional Record*. Much federal legislative history is available on Lexis Advance, Westlaw, and Bloomberg Law, both in general sources devoted to legislation and in topical sources. Some law libraries offer access to ProQuest Congressional and ProQuest Legislative Insight, both of which offer comprehensive access to federal legislative history.

Chapter 8

Administrative Law

I. Introduction

Administrative law is law made by agencies within the executive branch of government. With the exception of the relatively few agencies created by executive order,[1] Massachusetts state agencies derive their authority from enabling statutes enacted by the legislature. An agency may promulgate regulations,[2] adjudicate matters within its purview, and perform characteristically administrative functions such as conducting investigations or granting licenses. Law made by an agency is primary legal authority, like law made by a legislature or by a court.[3]

State agencies have narrower substantive focus than the legislature, which enacts statutes on a very broad spectrum of topics. This narrower focus allows an agency to gain expertise in a specific area.[4] For example, the Commonwealth's agencies include such specialized entities as the Division of Banks, the Department of Fish and Game, the Massachusetts Teachers Retirement System, the

---

1. In Massachusetts, some state agencies are created by executive order. For example, the Office of the Child Advocate was created by Executive Order No. 494 on February 28, 2008, pursuant to the authority of the Governor under Part 2, ch. 2, §1, art. 1, of the Commonwealth's Constitution, which makes the Governor the "supreme executive magistrate."

2. A "regulation" includes "the whole or any part of every rule, regulation, standard or other requirement of general application and future effect ... adopted by an agency to implement or interpret the law enforced or administered by it." Mass. Gen. Laws ch. 30A, §1(5).

3. *See Solomon v. School Comm. of Boston*, 395 Mass. 12, 17 (1985), and cases cited.

4. For a list of agencies within the Executive Offices as well as independent state agencies, see www.mass.gov/portal/government/state/. For an organizational chart of the executive branch, see www.mass.gov/bb/gaa/fy2009/app_09/ga_09/hcdefault.htm.

Department of Correction, and the Department of Industrial Accidents. Through enabling statutes, the legislature delegates to agencies the power to develop the law in the specific areas of their expertise. This delegation allows agencies to develop the law to a level of detail beyond that which is ordinarily practicable for a legislature. An agency accomplishes this goal by promulgating and implementing regulations and by conducting adjudicative proceedings.

Agency functions mirror functions of the legislative and judicial branches. An adjudicative proceeding before an agency is similar to a proceeding before a court, but is limited to matters within the purview of the agency.[5] Regulations are similar in some respects to legislation. Like legislation, a regulation may define statutory language or impose substantive or procedural requirements. The regulation, however, must be within the authority of the enabling statute and consistent with other legislation. Table 8-1 shows the statutory authority for one agency, the Board of Education, to promulgate regulations on student records, and portions of the agency's regulation defining terms of the statute.

An agency's enabling statute determines how the agency is organized and the scope of its authority. For example, the enabling statute for the Department of Mental Health is Mass. Gen. Laws ch. 19, §§ 1–24. Section 1 of the chapter identifies the department's area of concern and its general authority. Sections 2 through 5 state the titles and qualifications of the highest level of personnel in the department. Section 18 provides that the department "may from time to time adopt such rules and regulations as it deems necessary to carry out the provisions of this chapter, and may amend or repeal the same." Other provisions of the chapter give the department additional powers and duties. Table 8-2 shows the sections within Chapter 19 of the General Laws.

Procedures for rulemaking and adjudication by the Commonwealth's agencies are governed by the Massachusetts Administrative Procedure Act (APA), Chapter 30A of the General Laws.[6] The APA was enacted in 1954 to promote fairness and uniformity in the work of state agencies and uniformity in judicial review of agency action.[7] Chapter 30A does not apply to the Office of the Gov-

---

5. An "adjudicative proceeding" is "a proceeding before an agency in which the legal rights, duties or privileges of specifically named persons are required by constitutional right or by any provision of the General Laws to be determined after opportunity for an agency hearing." Mass. Gen. Laws ch. 30A, § 1(1).

6. Mass. Gen. Laws ch. 30A, §§ 2 and 3, address requirements of notice and hearing prior to adoption, amendment, or repeal of a regulation and provide for emergency regulations, which may remain in effect for a maximum of three months.

7. *See* Albert M. Sacks & William J. Curran, *Administrative Law*, 1954 B.C. Ann. Survey of Mass. Law 126, 127 (1955).

**Table 8-1. Example of Enabling Legislation and
Regulation Defining the Terms of a Statute**

Statute: Mass. Gen. Laws ch. 71, §§ 34D	Regulation: Portion of 603 CMR 23.02
The board of education shall adopt regulations relative to the maintenance, retention, duplication, storage and periodic destruction of student records by the public elementary and secondary schools of the commonwealth. Such rules and regulations shall provide that a parent or guardian of any pupil shall be allowed to inspect academic, scholastic, or any other records concerning such pupil which are kept or are required to be kept.	Parent shall mean a student's father or mother, or guardian, or person or agency legally authorized to act on behalf of the student in place of or in conjunction with the father, mother, or guardian. Any parent who by court order does not have physical custody of the student is considered a non-custodial parent for purposes of M.G.L. c. 71, § 34H and 603 CMR 23.00. This includes parents who by court order do not reside with or supervise the student, even for short periods of time.
	...
	The student record shall consist of the transcript and the temporary record, including all information recording and computer tapes, microfilm, microfiche, or any other materials regardless of physical form or characteristics concerning a student that is organized on the basis of the student's name or in a way that such student may be individually identified, and that is kept by the public schools of the Commonwealth. The term as used in 603 CMR 23.00 shall mean all such information and materials regardless of where they are located, except for the information and materials specifically exempted by 603 CMR 23.04.

Table 8-2. Sections of an Enabling Act in *Massachusetts General Laws*

Chapter 19 — Department of Mental Health

Section
1. Creation; powers of department and commissioner; safety symposium.
2. Commissioner; appointment; qualifications; appointments by commissioner; report; salary.
3. Deputy commissioner; appointment; duties; qualifications.
4. Assistant, deputy or associate commissioners; appointment; duties; qualifications.
5. Legal counsel.
6. Program for training of residents in psychiatry and other professional disciplines.
7. State facilities under department control; admission.
8. Superintendents or directors; vacancies; appointments; qualifications; officers.
8A. Boards of trustees for state hospitals.
9. Repealed by 1996 Mass. Acts, ch. 58, § 12.
10. Crimes committed by or upon persons on facility premises or persons in care of facility.
11. Mental health advisory council.
11A. Disclosure of financial interest in department contracts by human rights advisory committee members.
12. Community mental health services.
13. Community mental health area directors.
14. Community mental health area boards.
15. Duties and powers of area boards.
16. Development and maintenance of community mental health services.
17. Area advisory committees.
18. Rules and regulations
19. Residential or day care services; licenses.
20. Mental health facility employees; civil service exemption.
21. Interagency agreements with developmental services department.
22. Consultation of commissioner for behavioral health services for children.
23. Children's behavioral health research center; powers and duties; annual report.
24. Notification of parent or guardian of child receiving inpatient psychiatric services.

ernor or to certain other entities within the executive branch, and it applies only to a limited extent to another small group of entities.[8]

A public hearing with due notice is required in advance of adoption, amendment, or repeal of most regulations.[9] An agency may dispense with notice and hearing if "the agency finds that immediate adoption, amendment or repeal of a regulation is necessary for the preservation of the public health, safety or general welfare, and that observance of the requirements of notice and a public hearing would be contrary to the public interest."[10] In this situation, the regulation is adopted, amended, or repealed as an "emergency regulation," which may be effective for no more than three months.[11]

In addition to promulgating regulations, some agencies are empowered by their enabling legislation to conduct quasi-judicial proceedings to adjudicate matters within their purview. These proceedings must comply with the requirements of Mass. Gen. Laws ch. 30A, §§ 10–11, and with relevant regulations.[12] Although the APA requires an agency to keep an official record of a proceeding and to give reasons for its decision, the APA does not require agencies to publish their decisions.[13]

---

8. Under the APA, the term "agency" includes "any department, board, commission, division or authority of the state … authorized by law to make regulations or to conduct adjudicatory proceedings, but does not include the following: the legislative and judicial departments; the governor and council; military or naval boards, commissions or officials; the department of correction; the department of youth services; the parole board; the division of dispute resolution of the division of industrial accidents; the personnel administrator; the civil service commission; and the appellate tax board." Mass. Gen. Laws ch. 30A, § 1. Some of these entities, however, are subject to some requirements of the APA. *See* Mass. Gen. Laws ch. 30A, §§ 1A–1D, 37.

9. The notice and hearing requirement is set forth in Mass. Gen. Laws ch. 30A, § 2.

10. Mass. Gen. Laws ch. 30A, § 2.

11. An emergency regulation may remain in effect for longer than three months if during that period the agency gives notice, holds a public hearing, and files notice of compliance with the Secretary of State. Mass. Gen. Laws ch. 30A, § 2.

12. Mass. Gen. Laws ch. 30A, § 10A, prescribes the procedure for intervening in proceedings in which environmental damage is at issue. Standard Adjudicatory Rules of Practice and Procedure promulgated by the Executive Office of Administration and Finance are set forth beginning at 801 CMR 1.01.

13. Requirements for agency decisions are set forth in Mass. Gen. Laws ch. 30A, § 11, and in 801 CMR 1.01(11).

II. Sources for Massachusetts Administrative Law Research

The main sources for Massachusetts administrative law research are the Massachusetts APA, the various enabling statutes, the *Code of Massachusetts Regulations* (CMR), the *Massachusetts Register*, and reports of agency decisions. But the most valuable resource in administrative law research may be the agency itself. While statutes and regulations are relatively easy to find, be aware that there may be additional material that cannot be obtained through conventional research methods. For example, the agency may have an unpublished manual that outlines steps for processing a claim. Or the agency may have written guidelines for evaluating applications. Thus, in many situations your research will include talking to a representative of the agency to find out what material is available.

A. State Agency Regulations

1. *Code of Massachusetts Regulations*

The *Code of Massachusetts Regulations*, or CMR, is the official codification of Massachusetts administrative regulations.[14] It sets forth the current regulations promulgated by governmental bodies that are subject to the APA.[15]

In the CMR, each agency is assigned a three-digit number that prefaces its regulations. This number is referred to as the "title" of the regulations. Within the title, the agency's regulations are divided into chapters and then into sections. The standard format for citing a Massachusetts regulation uses title and section, but not chapter. For example, regulations relating to display of reflectorized license plates would be cited as 540 CMR 2.23, where 540 is the title of the CMR that has regulations of the Registry of Motor Vehicles, 2.00 is the chapter that has motor vehicle regulations, and section 2.23 is the section that has regulations concerning display of reflectorized license plates. Figure 8-1 shows an excerpt from the regulations of the Registry of Motor Vehicles in Title 540 of the CMR.

The official CMR is available only in print, in a multi-volume set published in loose-leaf format by the Secretary of the Commonwealth. The CMR is not annotated and does not have a general index.

---

14. For a detailed treatment of the CMR, see Chapter 6 in *Handbook of Legal Research in Massachusetts* (Mary Ann Neary & Ruth G. Matz eds., 3d ed., Mass. CLE 2009 & Supps. 2012 & 2015) and Alexander J. Cella, *Massachusetts Administrative Law and Practice* (Massachusetts Practice Series No. 38, 1986 and on Westlaw).

15. *See* Mass. Gen. Laws ch. 30A, §§ 5, 6A. For bodies that are exempt from the requirements of the APA, see Mass. Gen. L ch. 30A, § 1.

Figure 8-1. Excerpt from Regulations of the Registry of Motor Vehicles

540 CMR: REGISTRY OF MOTOR VEHICLES

540 CMR 2.00: MOTOR VEHICLE REGULATIONS

Section

2.05: Vehicle Registrations Requirements

2.06: Operator Licensing Requirements

2.07: Year of Manufacture Registration Plates

2.15: Licensing of Operators of School Buses

2.22: Markings on Commercial Vehicles

2.23: Display of Reflectorized License Plates

2.05: Vehicle Registrations Requirements

(1) Authority, Purpose and Scope. 540 CMR 2.05 is issued by the Registrar of Motor Vehicles under the authority of M.G.L. c. 16, § 9 and c. 90, §§ 2 and 31. In order to promote and protect the public safety, every motor vehicle and trailer operated, pushed, drawn, towed, or remaining in any way shall be in compliance with the registration requirements of M.G.L. c. 90, and 540 CMR 2.05 or 18.00....

(2) Applications for Registration and Powers of Attorney. Any person who desires to register a motor vehicle or trailer in the Commonwealth shall complete such application, and provide such information, as required by the Registrar. The application for registration may be signed on behalf of the applicant by a duly authorized attorney in fact acting under a valid power of attorney, provided the power of attorney or a copy thereof, duly authenticated, is filed with the application for registration

(3) Definitions. As used in 540 CMR 2.05, the following terms are defined as follows:

Ambulance, Antique Motor Car, Auto Home, House Trailer, Motorcycle, School Bus, Semi-trailer, and Trailer, shall have the meaning assigned to those terms in M.G.L. c. 90, § 1.

Apportionable Vehicle, is any motor vehicle which qualifies for registration under the International Registration Plan (IRP) authorized by M.G.L. c. 90, § 2, and which the Commonwealth joined effective January 1, 1994.

Bus, is any motor vehicle which is designed to transport 16 or more persons, including the driver, or meets the definition of Bus or Motor Bus under M.G.L. c. 90, § 1....

Source: Code of Massachusetts Regulations.

An unofficial, unannotated print version of the CMR is published by Matthew Bender[16] in a multi-volume, loose-leaf set called *Massachusetts Administrative Code.* This version has a guide volume that includes a subject index, a proposed regulations index, a regulation number index, and an emergency regulation index.[17] Many law libraries maintain only the guide volume, which is available separately from the rest of the set.

Unofficial versions of the CMR are also available electronically through commercial research services, including Lexis Advance, Westlaw, and Bloomberg Law, and to subscribers of the Social Law Library.[18] Portions of the CMR, posted by individual agencies, are available on the Massachusetts Trial Court Law Libraries website.[19] You can gain access to regulations by citation or through an online subject index compiled by the library staff.[20] The website also has an alphabetical list of the three-digit numbers assigned to agencies. Figure 8-2 shows a portion of the index to the CMR on the website of the Massachusetts Trial Court Law Libraries.

You can bypass the Massachusetts Trial Court Law Libraries website and locate regulations of some agencies on their own websites.[21] Individual regulations may also be ordered from the Massachusetts State Bookstore.[22]

---

16. Matthew Bender is part of the LexisNexis Group. Before 1995, this version was published by Weil Publishing Company and was called *Weil's Code of Massachusetts Regulations.*

17. This is the only source that has an index to emergency regulations.

18. The Social Law Library is a law library founded in 1803 by members of the Boston legal community. The General Court later passed legislation requiring the library to serve the research needs of the three branches of government in exchange for public funding. "Social" libraries were so named in a late-eighteenth-century statute authorizing people to join in a "Society or body politic" to operate a library. 1797 Mass. Acts 82. Social libraries were predecessors to the Commonwealth's public libraries, the first of which was not founded until 1848.

19. The seventeen Massachusetts Trial Court Law Libraries located across the state maintain a free online collection of legislative, judicial, executive, administrative, and municipal materials, as well as subject matter guides, legal forms, and historical documents. For information on the Massachusetts Trial Court Law Libraries, see http:// www.mass.gov/courts/case-legal-res/law-lib/.

20. The library's document delivery service will e-mail regulations not linked on the library's website. The index includes all sections, whether or not they are available on the web. The website for the index is http://www.mass.gov/courts/case-legal-res/ law-lib/laws-by-source/cmr/cmr-a-c-gen.html.

21. For example, the Board of Registration in Medicine makes its regulations available in PDF format on its website, http://www.mass.gov/eohhs/gov/departments/borim/.

22. The State Bookstore has physical locations in Boston, Springfield, and Fall River. Materials can also be ordered online. For more precise information, use the link to the State Bookstore at www.sec.state.ma.us.

Figure 8-2. Portion of CMR Index on Massachusetts Trial Court Law Libraries Website

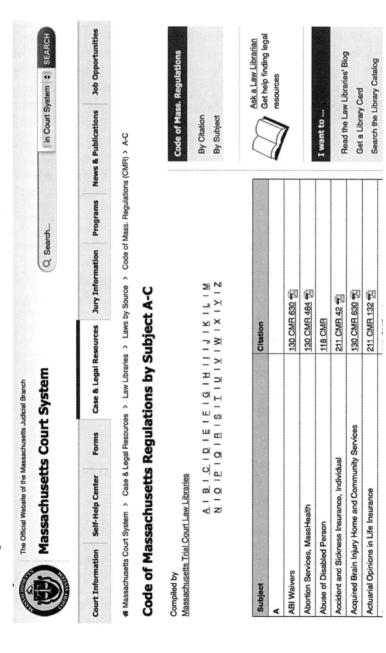

2. *Massachusetts Register*

The *Massachusetts Register*, which is published biweekly, publishes regulations, notices of public hearings and comment periods on proposed regulations and other notices of public interest, Opinions of the Attorney General and Executive Orders, and other material.[23] Pages from the *Massachusetts Register* are transferred directly to CMR binders to update the CMR. The *Massachusetts Register* is the main source for emergency regulations that do not become part of the CMR.

Every issue of the *Massachusetts Register* includes a cumulative index to regulatory changes in the CMR for the current year.[24] The *Massachusetts Register* is available widely in print, in public as well as law libraries, and in commercial research services.[25] Subscriptions are available through the State Bookstore.

B. Reports of Agency Decisions

When an agency adjudicates a matter, it must maintain a record of its decision. The APA requires that an agency make its decisions available to the public at its office.[26]

Because all Massachusetts agency decisions are not collected into a single, searchable database, locating decisions of some agencies may require considerable effort and persistence. The State Library of Massachusetts collects adjudicatory decisions of agencies in either print or electronic format, which can be located by searching the library's online index under the name of the issuing

---

23. Requirements relating to the *Massachusetts Register* are found in Mass. Gen. Laws ch. 30A, §6.

24. These indexes are not cumulated beyond a given year. Thus, many law libraries maintain a paper archive of the annual indexes.

25. The *Massachusetts Register* is available in Lexis Advance's "Massachusetts Register" source dating back to 1995. *Massachusetts Register* materials are available in Bloomberg Law's "Massachusetts Rulemaking" source. Although the *Massachusetts Register* itself is not available on Westlaw, its content appears in Westlaw's "Massachusetts Proposed & Adopted Regulations — Current" source, which contains proposed and recently enacted regulations for the past two years, and "Massachusetts Regulation Tracking," which contains summaries and status information for proposed and recently adopted regulations. Attorney General Opinions are available in Westlaw's "Massachusetts Attorney General Opinions" source.

26. This requirement is in Mass. Gen. Laws c. 30A, §6B.

agency.[27] The Social Law Library's Administrative Databases give subscribers access to some agency decisions in electronic form. Some agency decisions are also available in print to library subscribers. Table 8-3 shows administrative bodies[28] whose decisions are available to subscribers to the Social Law Library Administrative Databases.

Table 8-3. Decisions in Social Law Library Administrative Databases

Decisions	From Year
Alcoholic Beverages Control Commission	1990 to present
Appellate Tax Board	1986 to present
Bid Protest Decisions of the Attorney General	2005 to present
Board of Bar Overseers	1974 to present
Board of Conciliation and Arbitration	2000 to 2007
Board of Special Education Appeals	2007 to present
Board of Registration in Medicine	1989 to present
Civil Service Commission	2004 to present
Contributory Retirement Appeal Board	1993 to present
Department of Environmental Protection	1983 to present
Department of Industrial Accidents	1987 to present
Department of Public Health	2007 to 2013
Department of Public Utilities	1989 to 2011
Division of Insurance	1982 to present
Division of Labor Relations	1974 to present
Energy Facilities Siting Board	2000 to 2008
Housing Appeals Committee	1971 to present
Joint Labor Management Committee	1990 to present
Massachusetts Commission Against Discrimination	1983 to present
Office of the Attorney General	1985 to present
State Ethics Commission	1980 to present

Commercially published services, including Lexis Advance, Westlaw, and Bloomberg Law, have some agency decisions. Table 8-4 shows some additional sources that provide the full text of Massachusetts administrative decisions.

---

27. The State Library maintains a list of links to state agency decisions available online, see http://www.mass.gov/courts/case-legal-res/law-lib/laws-by-source/agency-decisions/.

28. Not all of these are agencies fully subject to the APA.

**Table 8-4. Additional Sources for Full Text of Decisions of
Massachusetts Agencies**

Appellate Tax Board
Massachusetts Appellate Tax Board Reporter (print, e-book after 2013 — published by Butterworth), with decisions beginning in 1982.
Lexis Advance (in "Massachusetts Appellate Tax Board Decisions"), with decisions beginning in 1979.
Westlaw (in "Massachusetts Taxation Administrative Decisions"), with decisions beginning in 1979.
Bloomberg Law (in "Appellate Tax Board," found within "Massachusetts Executive Office for Administration and Finance"), coverage not specified.

Bureau of Special Education Appeals
Massachusetts Special Education Reporter (print — published by Landlaw Specialty Publishers*), with decisions beginning in 1995.

Civil Service Commission
Massachusetts Civil Service Reporter (print — currently published by Landlaw),
with decisions beginning in 1989.
Lexis Advance (in "Massachusetts Civil Service Reporter"), with decisions beginning in 1992.

Department of Environmental Protection
*DEP Reporter: Massachusetts Department of Environmental Protection Adminis-
trative Law Decisions* (print — published by Landlaw), with decisions beginning in 1994.
Massachusetts Environmental Law Reports (decisions of the Department of Environmental Protection and its predecessor, Department of Environmental
Quality Engineering) (print — published by Atlantic), with decisions from
1983 to 1994.
Westlaw (in "Massachusetts Environmental Administrative Decisions"), with
decisions beginning in 1983.

Department of Industrial Accidents
Massachusetts Workers' Compensation Reports (print — published by Lexis-
Nexis), with decisions beginning in 1989.
Lexis Advance (in "Massachusetts Workers' Compensation Decisions"), with
decisions beginning in 1987.
Westlaw (in "Massachusetts Workers Compensation Administrative Deci-
sions"), with decisions beginning in 1987.

Labor Relations Commission
Massachusetts Labor Cases (print — published by Landlaw), with decisions beginning in 1974.
Lexis Advance (in "Massachusetts Labor Cases"), with decisions beginning in
1996.
Westlaw (in "Massachusetts Labor Relations Decisions"), with decisions beginning in 2000.

**Table 8-4. Additional Sources for Full Text of Decisions of
Massachusetts Agencies,** *continued*

Massachusetts Commission Against Discrimination
Massachusetts Discrimination Law Reporter (print — published by Landlaw),
with decisions beginning in 1979.
Lexis Advance (in "Massachusetts Commission Against Discrimination"), with
decisions beginning in 1979.
Westlaw (in "Massachusetts Commission Against Discrimination Decisions"),
with selective decisions beginning in 1999.

* Landlaw Specialty Publishers makes available to subscribers a key word searchable database of all the decisions in its print administrative reporters, going back to 1993 for most reporters. It also allows free searching of
its selective "Current Decisions" database.

C. Governor's Executive Orders and Opinions of the Attorney General

1. Executive Orders

Although the Governor's executive orders are not, strictly speaking, administrative law, they are primary legal authority issued by the executive branch,
so we address them in this chapter. The Governor does not have explicit power
under the Commonwealth's constitution to issue executive orders; rather, this
power is implied by the Governor's position within government as "supreme
executive magistrate."[29]

The *Massachusetts Register* publishes the text of executive orders, and the
State Library maintains a complete file and index of executive orders. The
website of the Massachusetts Trial Court Law Libraries has executive orders
online, indexed by date and by subject.[30] Figure 8-5 shows the links to executive orders issued by Governor Deval Patrick from March to December
2014.[31] As a convenience to users, the index includes information indicating
executive orders that were affected by later ones. For example, the index indicates that Executive Order No. 512 revokes and supersedes Executive Order
No. 439.

---

29. *See* Mass. Const. Part 2, ch. 2, §1, art. 1.
30. The website for the index is http://www.mass.gov/courts/case-legal-res/law-lib/
laws-by-source/exec/.
31. The site notes that the Governor's Office is the official source for executive orders.

Figure 8-3. Executive Orders Issued March 2014 to December 2014

🏛 Massachusetts Court System > Case & Legal Resources > Law Libraries > Laws by Source > Executive Orders > Executive Orders 550-date

Massachusetts Executive Orders 550-date

Governor Deval Patrick, 2007-15

Executive Order 550 (Mass. Register # 1257) 🗎

Issued March 12, 2014

Establishing a Task Force on Successful Women in the Workplace

Executive Order 551 (Mass. Register # 1267) 🗎

Issued July 28, 2014

Establishing a Commission to Study Compensation of Assistant District Attorneys and Public Defenders

Executive Order 552 (Mass. Register # 1276) 🗎

Issued November 20, 2014

Executive Order on Environmental Justice

Executive Order 553 (Mass. Register # 1277) 🗎

Issued December 10, 2014

Establishing the Massachusetts Percent for Art Program and the Public Art Commission

Executive Orders

By number
By subject

Ask a Law Librarian
Get help finding legal
resources

I want to ...

Read the Law Libraries' Blog
Get a Library Card
Search the Library Catalog
Renew a Book
Ask a Law Librarian
Get a Document
Find a Lawyer

Source: Massachusetts Trial Court Law Libraries, http://www.mass.gov/courts/case-legal-res/law-lib/laws-by-source/exec/eo550-599.html.

2. Attorney General Opinions

Opinions of the Attorney General also differ from standard agency regulations and decisions. Mass. Gen. Laws ch. 12, §§ 3, 6, and 9, give the Attorney General authority to render formal opinions and legal advice to constitutional officers, government agencies, and chambers and committees of the General Court. The Massachusetts Supreme Judicial Court ordinarily gives weight to formal opinions of the Attorney General on matters within the purview of that office.[32]

In print, opinions of the Attorney General are published in the *Massachusetts Register*. They are also available as slip opinions in various state libraries. Lexis Advance has Attorney General opinions going back to 1977. Westlaw has Attorney General opinions from 1976 to 2001. Older opinions are available on microfilm and microfiche from commercial providers. Some recent opinions are available on the website of the Office of the Attorney General.[33]

III. Using Massachusetts Administrative Law in Legal Problem Solving

Administrative agencies act in a wide range of subject areas. Thus, you should ordinarily consider the possibility that there is some administrative law relevant to your problem. When you find a statute that is relevant to a problem, ask whether the legislature has delegated to an administrative agency the power to promulgate regulations or adjudicate matters governed by the statute and, if so, locate, update, and evaluate relevant regulations or agency decisions.

A. Finding an Entry Point to Regulations

An annotated code may provide an entry point for regulations because annotated codes include cross-references to other primary sources, including regulations. While a cross-reference in an annotated code may provide an entry point, you cannot rely on the editors to identify all relevant regulations. You must ascertain for yourself which, if any, regulations are relevant to your problem.

Moreover, in order to use a statute as an entry point to regulations, you must first know that this particular statute is relevant. Some enabling statutes

---

32. *See, e.g., Andrews v. Civil Serv. Comm'n*, 446 Mass. 611, 617 n. 14 (2006).
33. The website is www.mass.gov/ago/government-resources/ags-opinions/.

give agencies very broad discretion to regulate. Given this broad discretion, an enabling statute may not always make apparent the specific subject matter of regulations promulgated under its authority, and the editors of an annotated code may not include cross-references to all relevant regulations. Thus, you may need to begin your search for regulations in sources other than an annotated code.

For example, 520 CMR 5.15 regulates recreational climbing walls. The stated authority for the regulations in 520 CMR 5.00 and following is Mass. Gen. Laws ch. 140, § 205A, which states, in part, that

> the words 'amusement device' shall mean a mechanical ride or device constructed and designed to carry 1 or more persons for entertainment or amusement purposes and which is powered by means of internal combustion or electrical energy; provided, however, that the commissioner of public safety, hereinafter called the commissioner shall have the discretion to further define an amusement device operated under this section.

If you were to come across Mass. Gen. Laws ch. 140, § 205A, while researching a problem involving a climbing wall, you might very well pass over this statute. Although the statute gives the commissioner discretion to "further define an amusement device," the statute itself mentions only mechanical devices. The only cross-references to the CMR in the statute's annotations on either Lexis Advance or Westlaw refer to "Ferris wheels, carousels, inclined railways" and "amusement devices." Thus, even if you were to find this statute, you might fail to identify it as an entry point to regulations relating to climbing walls.

Fortunately, there are other ways to locate a potentially relevant regulation. The most efficient way is to get a citation from a colleague or from a secondary source. Practice materials, including continuing legal education materials, are particularly useful entry points to state regulations. Once you have the citation to a regulation, you can look it up in the print CMR or in an online source.

On Lexis Advance, Westlaw, and Bloomberg Law, you can retrieve a regulation by conducting a full-text search in their Massachusetts regulations sources. For this purpose, natural-language searching is generally more effective than terms-and-connectors searching because terms-and-connectors searching requires greater precision, and it is difficult to predict the precise language and syntax of a regulation.

You can also find the citation to a regulation by looking up search terms in a subject index. Although the official print CMR does not have a subject index, your library may have the guide volume that is part of the Matthew Bender

Massachusetts Administrative Code set. This volume includes a subject index based on the table of contents of the CMR. Online, you can browse the index on the website of the Massachusetts Trial Court Law Libraries. This index has the names of issuing agencies as well as some subject headings. The index provides links to some regulations; the library's document delivery service will e-mail or fax other regulations free of charge.

If you know which agency issued the regulations, you can find an entry point by browsing the table of contents in the print CMR or online through the State Library's website or one of the commercial services. At the beginning of each volume of the print CMR is an alphabetical list of agencies that shows, for each agency, the agency's three-digit number and the volume that contains regulations promulgated by that agency. This information will lead you to a specific table of contents for the agency, which you can browse to find potentially relevant regulations. On Lexis Advance, Westlaw, and Bloomberg Law, the CMR table of contents allows you to use your browser's "find" function to search for the agency name.

B. Reading Regulations

Finding a potentially relevant regulation is just the first step. You must read the regulation carefully to assess first *whether* it applies to the problem you are working on and, if so, *how* it applies.

When you work with regulations, draw on your skills in statutory analysis. First, read the regulation slowly and carefully. Be mindful of the overall structure of the regulation because that can have important implications for its meaning. You may need to outline the regulation or create a flow chart to fully understand how the provisions of a regulation relate to each other. Be mindful especially of "and" and "or." These short words are very powerful indicators of the relationships of words and phrases within a regulation.

Note words or phrases that are vague or ambiguous. Check both the beginning of the section you are working with and the beginning of the agency's regulations for defined terms. Also, check the table of contents for related regulations.

C. Updating Regulations and Locating Historical Versions

Whenever you work with a legal primary source, you must update it to make sure it is still valid. When you work with regulations, you must be careful to have the appropriate *version* of the regulation. If you are problem solving prospectively, for example, in a situation in which you are advising a client who is planning to open a gym that includes a climbing wall, you must identify the version of the regulation that is in effect at present and track regulatory changes into the future. If you are problem solving retrospectively, for example, if your client's application for license renewal was denied on the ground of past non-compliance with regulations, you must locate a historical version of the regulations—the version that was in effect at the relevant time in the past— in order to figure out whether your client has grounds for appeal.

1. Updating Regulations Using Lexis Advance, Westlaw, and Bloomberg Law

Lexis Advance, Westlaw, and Bloomberg Law provide frequent updates of the CMR. The screen that shows the full text of a regulation will show the date through which the regulation is current. Emergency regulations are not included in the CMR, so searching the appropriate CMR source on one of the commercial services will not turn up emergency regulations that affect the regulation you are working with.

To locate emergency regulations on Lexis Advance, search the "Massachusetts Register" source. You can also track regulations on Lexis Advance through the "MA State Regulation Tracking" source. To find emergency regulations on Westlaw, use the "Massachusetts Proposed and Adopted Regulations" source, which provides the full text of proposed and recently adopted regulations. To find emergency regulations on Bloomberg Law, use the "Massachusetts Rule-making" source, which provides the full text of proposed, final, emergency, temporary, and interim rules.

2. Updating Regulations in Print

The print CMR is continually updated by inserting pages of the *Massachusetts Register* into the proper place in the loose-leaf binders. Thus, when it is appropriately maintained, the CMR is updated to the date of the most recent *Massachusetts Register*.[34] There is an exception to this, however. Emergency regulations are not collated with the regulations they affect, although they may be filed together in one of the loose-leaf binders. Thus, to be certain that there is no emergency regulation that affects the regulation you are working with, you must use the emergency regulations index in the guide volume of the *Mas-*

---

34. An emergency regulation is effective when it is filed with the Secretary of the Commonwealth. A non-emergency regulation is effective upon publication in the *Massachusetts Register* unless a later effective date is required by statute or stated in the regulation. Mass. Gen. Laws ch. 30A, §6.

sachusetts Administrative Code set or skim through the last three months of
the *Massachusetts Register* (because an emergency regulation may be effective
for only ninety days).

3. Finding Historical Versions

If your problem involves facts that were fixed in the past, the current version
of a regulation may not be applicable. To determine whether the current version applies to your problem, first identify the effective date of the regulation.
In the print CMR, the lower left-hand corner of each page shows a date. If
that date is in 1995 or later, this indicates the date the regulation was published
in the *Massachusetts Register*. This is the effective date of the regulation, unless
a different effective date appears in parentheses next to that date. If the date
in the lower left-hand corner is before 1995, it may not be the effective date
of the regulation. In this situation, you should consult the Regulations Division
of the Secretary of the Commonwealth to find out the effective date of the
regulation.

Many law libraries, including the Massachusetts Trial Court Law Libraries,
maintain older editions of the CMR and superseded pages. But using the annual
Cumulative Tables and the full run of the *Massachusetts Register* is the most
authoritative and comprehensive way to find historical Massachusetts regulations. The Regulations Division of the Secretary of the Commonwealth provides
assistance in tracking down regulations that are no longer in effect.

Documents in the Massachusetts regulations sources on Lexis Advance,
Westlaw, and Bloomberg Law do not show each regulation's effective date. You
must consult the print CMR or the Regulations Division to determine the effective date. Lexis Advance and Westlaw offer fairly recent historical versions
of the CMR. When viewing a CMR section on Lexis Advance, click on "Archived
code versions" to see recent versions of that section. On Westlaw, the "Massachusetts Historical Regulations" source shows recent annual versions of the
CMR. Bloomberg Law does not currently offer historical versions of the CMR.

IV. Federal Administrative Law

The agencies of the federal government have powers analogous to those of
Massachusetts agencies. Like Massachusetts agencies, federal agencies promulgate
and implement regulations and decide matters within their purview. Agencies
such as the Civil Rights Division of the Department of Justice, the Internal Rev-
enue Service, and the U.S. Fish and Wildlife Service are invaluable parts of the
executive branch. The federal APA is codified at 5 U.S.C. § 551 et seq.

A. *Code of Federal Regulations*

Federal regulations are published by the Government Publishing Office (GPO) in the *Code of Federal Regulations* (CFR). This is a codification of regulations issued by federal agencies.

Regulations in the CFR are organized by agency and subject. The titles of CFR do not necessarily correspond to the titles of the *United States Code* (USC), although some topics do fall under the same title number. For instance, Title 7 in both CFR and USC pertain to agriculture, but Title 11 of USC addresses bankruptcy, while the same title in the CFR deals with federal elections.

Like Massachusetts regulations, federal regulations are available in print and electronically. The print CFR is widely available in law libraries as well as in government and public libraries. The CFR is also available through several different free internet resources. Researchers can find the CFR on FDsys, the GPO's online source for official documents from all three branches of government.[35] FDsys is scheduled to be replaced in 2017 with govinfo.gov, which was in beta testing as this book was being finalized. The govinfo.gov beta site also carries the CFR. You can find an unofficial version of the CFR at e-CFR.[36] The CFR is also available on Lexis Advance, Westlaw, and Bloomberg Law.

B. *Federal Register*

New regulations and proposed changes to existing regulations are published first in the *Federal Register*, the federal analogue to the *Massachusetts Register*. The *Federal Register* is the first print source to publish regulations in their final form when they are adopted (that is, before they are codified in the CFR). In addition to providing the text of regulations, the *Federal Register* also contains notices of hearings, responses to public comments on proposed regulations, and helpful tables and indexes. It is published almost every weekday, with continuous pagination throughout the year. This means that page numbers in the thousands are common. The online version of the *Federal Register* is available through FDsys and the beta version of govinfo.gov, and is available on Lexis Advance, Westlaw, and Bloomberg Law.

---

35. The website is www.gpo.gov/fdsys. From 2009 through 2011, the GPO migrated the information on its prior GPO Access system to the current Federal Digital System (FDsys). The GPO shut down GPO Access in 2012. For a brief history of how the GPO has provided electronic access to official government publications, see http://www.gpo.gov/pdfs/fdsys-info/FDsys_FAQ.pdf.

36. The website is www.ecfr.gov.

C. Working with the CFR

1. Finding Potentially Relevant Federal Regulations

To find potentially relevant federal regulations, use your general research process. As with other primary sources, the most efficient place to start is with a known citation or with a secondary source. Once you have a citation, you can look it up in print or online in a number of sources.

You can also begin your search for regulations in an annotated code that has references to related regulations for each statute. After finding a statute on point, review the annotations following the statutory language for cross-references to relevant regulations.

In print, you can use the general index to the CFR, published by the GPO. You can find the citation to a regulation by looking up your research terms or the relevant agency's name. Consider using the index to the CFR published by West, which is more comprehensive than the GPO index.

Online, FDsys and the govinfo.gov beta site allow you to search any source by key word as well as by citation. More search options are available on e-CFR, which allows terms-and-connectors searching in addition to searching by key word. Lexis Advance and Westlaw both allow natural-language and term-and-connectors searching of their CFR sources. Bloomberg Law allows terms-and-connectors searches of its CFR source. You can also obtain the text of a regulation by typing its citation in the appropriate field.

2. Updating Federal Regulations

After looking up and carefully reading a regulation, update it. Lexis Advance, Westlaw, and Bloomberg Law keep their CFR sources relatively current. In addition, the unofficial version of the CFR at e-CFR is current within two business days and displays links to amendments that have been promulgated but have not yet taken effect. But whenever you use a topical code, like the CFR, you should carefully update with a chronologically organized publication, like the *Federal Register*.

Print CFR volumes are updated annually, with specific titles updated each quarter. Titles 1 through 16 are updated as of January 1,[37] Titles 17 through 27 are updated as of April 1, Titles 28 through 41 are updated as of July 1, and Titles 42 through 50 are updated as of October 1. These updates may only become available months after the schedule indicates. Each year, the covers of

---

37. The exception is Title 3, "The President," which includes executive orders. Unlike other CFR titles, it is not updated annually, but compiles orders for a single year.

CFR volumes are a different color, which makes it easy to tell whether a print volume has been updated. If no changes were made in a particular volume for the new year, a cover with the new color is pasted on the old volume.

To update a federal regulation in print or on FDsys, begin with a small booklet or the database called *List of CFR Sections Affected* (LSA). As its name suggests, LSA lists all sections of CFR that have been affected by recent agency action. LSA provides page references to *Federal Register* issues where action affecting a section of CFR is included. If the section you are researching is not listed in LSA, then it has not been changed since its annual revision. LSA is published monthly and is available by browsing the list of publications on FDsys.

Final updating requires reference to a table at the back of the *Federal Register* called "CFR Parts Affected During [the current month]." (Do not confuse this table with the "CFR Parts Affected in this [Current] Issue" located in the Contents at the beginning of each issue.) Refer to this table in each *Federal Register* for the last day of each month for all the months between the most recent monthly LSA issue and the current date. Also check the most recent issue of the *Federal Register* for the present month. The table contains more general information (whether a "part" has been affected, not a "section"), but will note changes made since the most recent LSA. On FDsys users can browse the "List of CFR Sections Affected" to find final and proposed rules published in the Federal Register within the past twenty-four hours, week, month, or within a specific date range.

The updating described above is similar to using pocket parts to update research in a digest. You can update federal regulations online with *Shepard's* and KeyCite. Bloomberg Law's BCite does not apply to regulations.

D. Decisions of Federal Agencies

Like Massachusetts agencies, federal agencies hold quasi-judicial hearings to decide cases that arise under the agencies' regulations. Some of these decisions are published in reporters specific to each agency, for example, *Decisions and Orders of the National Labor Relations Board*. Increasingly, agency decisions are available on agency websites and from Lexis Advance, Westlaw, and Bloomberg Law.

E. Decisions of Courts Reviewing Agency Action

The methods of case research explained in Chapters 4 and 5 will lead you to opinions in which the judiciary reviewed decisions of federal agencies. As with statutes, you can use the citation to a federal regulation in KeyCite to locate cases that cite it.[38]

F. Other Federal Administrative Materials

In addition to regulations and decisions, federal agencies issue other publications such as explanations, guidelines, manuals, and handbooks. Some of these publications are generally available. You may be able to obtain others from the agency itself. As with Massachusetts administrative law, when you are researching federal administrative law, the agency itself is a valuable resource.

---

38. BCite currently does not provide citing references for federal regulations.

Chapter 9

Constitutions

I. Introduction

The Massachusetts Constitution of 1780 may be the "oldest written working constitution in the world."[1] It has been amended 120 times, but is still in force. Drafted by John Adams, the Massachusetts Constitution was the principal model for the United States Constitution and thus, by extension, for the constitutions of other states.[2]

The Massachusetts Constitution has three parts: the Preamble; Part the First: A Declaration of the Rights of the Inhabitants of the Commonwealth of Massachusetts; and Part the Second: The Frame of Government. A very old document, the constitution is not subdivided consistently. For example, Part 1 is subdivided only into articles, while Part 2 is subdivided into chapters, some of which are first subdivided into sections, and then articles. Articles of Amendment are designated with Roman numerals.

A. The Preamble

The Preamble reflects the classical liberal political philosophy of the time when it was drafted. It declares that the purpose of government "is to secure the existence of the body politic, to protect it, and to furnish the individuals who compose it with the power of enjoying in safety and tranquility their natural rights." It goes on to state that "the body politic is formed by a voluntary association of individuals; it is a social compact." When government does not

---

1. Paul C. Reardon, *The Massachusetts Constitution Marks a Milestone*, 12 Publius 45 (1982).
2. *See* Charles H. Baron, *The Supreme Judicial Court in its Fourth Century: Meeting the Challenge of the "New Constitutional Revolution,"* 77 Mass. L. Rev. 35, 37 (1992).

achieve its purpose, "the people have a right to alter the government, and to take measures necessary for their safety, prosperity, and happiness."

B. The Declaration of Rights

The Declaration of Rights has thirty articles. It includes many rights present in the Bill of Rights of the U.S. Constitution, such as freedom of religion, freedom of the press, freedom from cruel or usual punishment, and the right to trial by jury. The Declaration of Rights also secures the rights of equal protection and to due process of law. The final article of the Declaration provides for separation of legislative, executive, and judicial powers.

The text of the Massachusetts Constitution, as amended, creates individual rights that are more extensive than rights under the U.S. Constitution. For example, the first article of the Massachusetts Constitution, which originally stated, "All men are born free and equal, and have certain natural, essential, and unalienable rights...." was annulled by Amendments, Article CVI, ratified in 1976, which adopted the following language: "All people are born free and equal and have certain natural, essential, and unalienable rights.... Equality under the law shall not be denied or abridged because of sex, race, color, creed or national origin."

Since the late 1970s, the Supreme Judicial Court of Massachusetts has issued a number of decisions recognizing a broader scope of individual rights under the Declaration of Rights than under cognate provisions of the U.S. Constitution.[3] These decisions include, among others, a 1985 decision recognizing an exclusionary rule under Article XIV[4] and a 1978 decision interpreting the right of free speech in Article XVI as protecting the freedom of expression of a nude dancer.[5] Perhaps the best known decision of the Supreme Judicial Court

---

3. *See id.* at 38–44 and authorities cited. The Supreme Judicial Court was explicit about this view in *Goodridge v. Dep't of Pub. Health*, 440 Mass. 309 (2003), where it stated:

> The Massachusetts Constitution protects matters of personal liberty against government incursion as zealously, and often more so, than does the Federal Constitution, even where both Constitutions employ essentially the same language.... Fundamental to the vigor of our Federal system of government is that "state courts are absolutely free to interpret state constitutional provisions to accord greater protection to individual rights than do similar provisions of the United States Constitution."

440 Mass. at 328 (citations omitted).
4. *See Commonwealth v. Ford*, 394 Mass. 421 (1985).
5. *See Commonwealth v. Sees*, 374 Mass. 534 (1978).

under the Declaration of Rights is *Goodridge v. Department of Public Health*,[6] which held that provisions of the Declaration of Rights and other provisions of the Massachusetts Constitution afford to same-sex couples the right to marry.[7]

C. The Frame of Government

The final part of the constitution, The Frame of Government, devotes a chapter to each of the three major divisions of the Commonwealth's government: the legislative, the executive, and the judiciary. As originally adopted, Part 2 included Chapter IV, which provided that delegates to the U.S. Congress would be elected by the state legislature. This provision was annulled by the adoption of the Constitution of the United States on July 26, 1788.

Chapter V, entitled "The University at Cambridge, and Encouragement of Literature, Etc.," shows the importance the Commonwealth accords to education. The principle that education is the foundation of democratic society is stated explicitly in Section II of Chapter V, which provides, in part,

> Wisdom and knowledge, as well as virtue, diffused generally among the body of the people, being necessary for the preservation of their rights and liberties; and as these depend on spreading the opportunities and advantages of education ... among the different orders of the people, it shall be the duty of legislatures and magistrates, in all future periods of this commonwealth, to cherish the interests of literature and the sciences, and all seminaries of them; especially the university at Cambridge, public schools and grammar schools in the towns....

In 1993, the Supreme Judicial Court held that this provision of the Massachusetts Constitution imposes a duty on the Commonwealth to provide an education for all its children.[8]

Chapter 6 concludes Part 2, setting forth miscellaneous provisions relating to oaths of office, the form and execution of writs, the continuation of laws in effect prior to adoption of the constitution, and habeas corpus. This chapter also included a procedure for amending the constitution, which itself has been amended, most recently by Amendment, Article XLVIII, ratified in 1918. Table

---

6. 440 Mass. 309 (2003).

7. The U.S. Supreme Court adopted reasoning in *Goodridge* in *Obergefell v. Hodges*. *See* 135 S. Ct. 2584, 2599 (2015).

8. *McDuffy v. Sec. of the Exec. Off. of Educ.*, 415 Mass. 545, 548 (1993).

9-1 shows an outline of Part 2 of the Massachusetts Constitution, which establishes the "Frame of Government."

Table 9-1. Outline of Part 2 of the Massachusetts Constitution

Chapter I — The Legislative Power
Section I   —   The General Court
Section II   —   The Senate
Section III —   The House of Representatives

Chapter II — Executive Power
Section I   —   The Governor
Section II   —   Lieutenant Governor
Section III —   Council, and the Manner of Settling Elections by the Legislature
Section IV   —   Secretary, Treasurer, Commissary, etc.

Chapter III — Judiciary Power

Chapter IV — Delegates to Congress
(annulled by adoption of the Constitution of the United States)

Chapter V — The University at Cambridge, and Encouragement of Literature, etc.
Section I   —   The University
Section II   —   The Encouragement of Literature, etc.

Chapter VI — Oaths and Subscriptions; Incompatibility of and Exclusion from Office ... Provision for a Future Revisal of the Constitution, etc.

D. Articles of Amendment

The Massachusetts Constitution of 1780 has 120 Articles of Amendment. Among these are Article II, which gives the legislature power to constitute municipal governments; Article XI, which safeguards religious freedom; and Article LXXXVIII, relating to the industrial development of cities and towns.[9]

E. Citation to the Massachusetts Constitution

Section 2.13 of the *Style Manual* prepared by the Massachusetts Office of the Reporter of Decisions states, "The Massachusetts Constitution will be cited in the same manner as appears in recent volumes of Massachusetts Reports"

---

9. For a table setting out a numerical listing of each of the Articles of Amendment with the year of its ratification by the voters, see Exhibit 1A in Chapter 1 of *Handbook of Legal Research in Massachusetts* (Mary Ann Neary & Ruth G. Matz eds., 3d ed., Mass. CLE 2009 & Supps. 2012 & 2015).

and provides common examples.[10] Examples from the *Style Manual* of citations to the Massachusetts Constitution and its Articles of Amendment are given in Table 9-2.

Table 9-2. Citation to Massachusetts Constitution and Articles of Amendment under the Massachusetts *Style Manual*

art. 48, The Initiative, II, § 3

art. 12 of the Declaration of Rights of the Massachusetts Constitution ("Massachusetts Declaration of Rights" acceptable)

art. 114 of the Amendments to the Massachusetts Constitution

art. 63, § 5, of the Amendments to the Massachusetts Constitution, as amended by art. 90 of the Amendments

art. 16 of the Declaration of Rights, as amended by art. 77 of the Amendments to the Massachusetts Constitution

Pt. II, c. 1, § 2, art. 8, of the Constitution of the Commonwealth

art. 101, § 3, of the Amendments to the Massachusetts Constitution

Source: *Style Manual* Prepared by Massachusetts Office of the Reporter of Decisions (2015–16).

General citation manuals require more consistent citation of the constitution and its Articles of Amendment. Table 9-3 shows how the constitution is cited under the rules in general citation manuals.

Table 9-3. Citation to Massachusetts Constitution and Articles of Amendment under the *ALWD Guide* and *Bluebook*

Mass. Const. pt. 1, art. V.

Mass. Const. pt. 2, ch. I, § II, art. II.

Mass. Const. amend. art. LXVIII.

Mass. Const. pt. 1, art. XVI (as amended by amend. art. LXVII).

Source: *ALWD Guide to Legal Citation* Rule 13 (5th ed. 2014); *The Bluebook* Rule 11 (20th ed. 2015).

---

10. The *Style Manual* is used by the justices of the Supreme Judicial Court, their law clerks, and the staff of the Office of the Reporter of Decisions. Online access to the Style Manual is at http://www.mass.gov/courts/docs/sjc/docs/reporter-of-decisions-style-guide.pdf.

II. Using the Massachusetts Constitution in Legal Problem Solving

A. Ask Whether the Massachusetts Constitution Applies

The Massachusetts Constitution addresses a broader range of topics than does the U.S. Constitution, so be attuned to the possibility that a provision of the state constitution applies to the problem you are working on. For example, what might appear at first to be a garden-variety land transfer could implicate a provision of the constitution. Article XCVIII of the Amendments provides that the people

> have the right to clean air and water, freedom from excessive and un-necessary noise, and the natural, scenic, historic, and esthetic qualities of their environment; and the protection of the people in their right to the conservation, development and utilization of the agricultural, mineral, forest, water, air and other natural resources is hereby de-clared to be a public purpose.

Under this provision, a two-thirds vote of each house of the legislature is required to divert to other purposes lands taken or used for the above purposes. Thus, if there is a possibility that the land is being used this way, you would have to research whether this provision of the constitution applies to your transaction.

B. Locate a Relevant Provision

If your preliminary research in a secondary source gives you the citation to a provision of the constitution, go directly to the text. The Massachusetts Constitution is available in electronic and print sources, in annotated and unannotated versions. Some versions are "integrated" — that is, the language of a given provision is updated to reflect amendments to the date the source was published. Some versions are "unintegrated," retaining the original language of amended provisions and providing references or hyperlinks to amending language. Thus, the first step in working with the constitution is to check whether the version you are using is an integrated or unintegrated version.

In print, West publishes the constitution in four volumes that are shelved near the end of the set of *Massachusetts General Laws*. These volumes include two versions of the constitution: one annotated and one unannotated. The annotated version has research aids similar to those that accompany sections of the *General Laws*,[11] including summaries of cases interpreting or applying provisions of the constitution. The unannotated version is in the fourth volume of the set. Both versions are unintegrated, but reference the reader to relevant Articles of Amendment. The four-volume set includes an index to the constitution.

The print constitution published by LexisNexis in the *Annotated Laws of Massachusetts* (ALM) is integrated. ALM publishes the constitution in a single volume that is shelved near the end of the ALM set. The volume includes an index to the constitution. In a note at the beginning of the volume, the publisher explains the system it uses to identify provisions that were changed or added by Articles of Amendment. An appendix to the volume sets forth the constitution as it was originally enacted.

Online, an unintegrated version of the constitution is available on the website of the state legislature.[12] This version uses hyperlinks to link to relevant Articles of Amendment. The state legislature's version also lists proposed Articles of Amendment that were rejected by popular vote.

Lexis Advance and Westlaw have integrated versions of the Massachusetts Constitution. Bloomberg Law has an unintegrated version. On Lexis Advance, use the "Explore Content" feature and select state law and then Massachusetts to get access to an annotated version of the Massachusetts Constitution, with table of contents. You can use the general search box to retrieve a specific section of the constitution by citation, or conduct a full-text search for relevant provisions, filtering your result appropriately. In Westlaw, you can browse to an annotated version of the Massachusetts Constitution by selecting "State Materials," "Massachusetts," and then "Massachusetts Statutes and Court Rules." This version also has a table of contents. If you have the citation to the provision you are looking for, you can use the global search box retrieve the provision. You can also locate relevant provisions of the Massachusetts Constitution by conducting a full-text search and narrowing your result appropriately. Bloomberg Law has an unintegrated, unannotated version of the Massachusetts Constitution that you can access by navigating to Massachusetts materials and then to "Mass. Legislative." This version has a browsable table of contents. A general full-text search will retrieve relevant provisions of the constitution relevant to a specific problem.

---

11. Chapter 6 explains how to use an annotated code.
12. The address is https://malegislature.gov/Laws/Constitution.

C. Read the Provision and Cases Interpreting It

As with a statute, be sure to read the provision of the constitution carefully to make a preliminary assessment whether and how it applies to your client's problem. Then, confirm your assessment by analyzing cases interpreting the provision. Constitutions are heavily interpreted because by their nature their provisions tend to be more general than statutes. Because an annotated code—in print or online—provides references to interpretive materials, it is a particularly useful tool when a problem involves a constitutional provision. The process of using an annotated code in this context is virtually identical to the process of using an annotated code in statutory research discussed in Chapter 6.

III. Researching the United States Constitution

The text of the United States Constitution is available in multiple sources in print and online. In print, both the *United States Code Annotated* (published by West) and the *United States Code Service* (published by LexisNexis) include annotated versions of the U.S. Constitution as a convenience for researchers. Both MGLA and ALM include the U.S. Constitution, although only ALM has annotations of Massachusetts cases interpreting it.

Online, annotated versions of the U.S. Constitution are available on Lexis Advance and Westlaw. An unannotated version is available on Bloomberg Law. The U.S. Constitution is available on many websites. For example, the website of the U.S. Congress provides free online access to The *Constitution of the United States of America: Analysis and Interpretation* (popularly known as the Constitution Annotated).[13] This publication contains the text of the U.S. Constitution as well as legal analysis and interpretation, based primarily on Supreme Court case law. This resource is also available as a free app for the iPhone and iPad.[14]

---

13. The address is https://www.congress.gov/constitution-annotated/.
14. Go to https://itunes.apple.com/us/app/u.s.-constitution-analysis/id6922600 32?mt=8. As of this writing, an Android version is under development.

Chapter 10

Law of Evidence and Rules of Court, Including Rules of Professional Conduct

I. Introduction

Court rules govern the practice of litigation from the filing of initial pleadings through the final appeal. Rules dictate litigation details ranging from the page length of briefs[1] to the precedential weight of unpublished opinions.[2] In Massachusetts, court rules also govern professional conduct of lawyers[3] and admission to the bar, including details relating to the bar examination.[4] Thus, even lawyers who do not litigate must know how to locate and use court rules.

The Supreme Judicial Court (SJC) promulgates rules affecting all the courts in the Commonwealth and the practice of law, pursuant to statutory authority in Chapter 211, Section 3 of the Massachusetts General Laws, which gives the SJC responsibility for "general superintendence of all courts of inferior jurisdiction," including the power to issue "such orders, directions and rules as may be necessary or desirable for the furtherance of justice ... and the securing of their proper and efficient administration." Thus, the SJC has adopted rules of civil, criminal, and appellate procedure. The SJC has also adopted Supreme Judicial Court Rules, which include rules that apply specifically to proceedings before the SJC and rules regulating the legal profession. Lower courts, with the approval of the SJC, have adopted rules relating specifically to proceedings before them.

The SJC has not, however, adopted rules of evidence. In Massachusetts courts, unlike in the federal courts and the courts of 42 states, the law governing

---

1. Mass. R. App. P. 16(h).
2. Mass. App. Ct. R. 1:28.
3. S.J.C. Rule 3:07.
4. S.J.C. Rule 3:01.

evidence is drawn from common law, statutes, and procedural rules instead of from a codified body of rules of evidence. Researching the law of evidence is addressed in this chapter because you would reasonably expect to find this topic in a chapter on rules. This chapter addresses evidence law first and then discusses conventional court rules.

II. Evidence

Because evidence law is uncodified in Massachusetts, researchers have traditionally relied heavily on treatises to lead them to relevant principles of law.[5] With the adoption of the Federal Rules of Evidence in 1975, the SJC established a committee to draft rules of evidence for Massachusetts. In 1982, the SJC rejected the Proposed Rules.[6] Nonetheless, the court stated that "the Proposed Rules have substantial value as a comparative standard in the continued and historic role of the courts in developing principles of law relating to evidence," and invited parties to cite the Proposed Rules "wherever appropriate."[7] Thus, the Proposed Rules were frequently cited by parties and mentioned by courts.[8]

In 2008, the SJC first published the *Massachusetts Guide to Evidence* (the *Guide*).[9] The statement of the SJC that prefaces the *Guide* recommends its use, but states that its "recommendation is not to be interpreted as an adoption of a set of rules of evidence, nor a predictive guide to the development of the common

---

5. Two particularly influential treatises on Massachusetts law of evidence are Mark S. Brodin & Michael Avery, *Handbook of Massachusetts Evidence 2016 Edition* (Wolters Kluwer 2015) and Hon. William G. Young, John R. Pollets, & Christopher Poreda, *Evidence 3d* (*Massachusetts Practice Series*, Vols. 19–20, West 2015).

6. The SJC's announcement gave several reasons for rejecting the Proposed Rules, including that 1) there would be a need to coordinate with the legislature to amend or repeal many statutes relating to admissibility or effect of evidence, 2) many rules departed from principles in the Federal Rules of Evidence, and 3) some rules were subject to substantive criticism. The announcement appeared in *Massachusetts Lawyers Weekly* at 11 Mass. Law. Wkly. 457 (Jan. 10, 1983).

7. *Id.*

8. *See, e.g., Suffolk Constr. Co. v. Div. of Capital Asset Mgmt.*, 449 Mass. 444, 452 n.12 (2007) (proposed rule 402(d)(6)); *Ruszcyk v. Sec'y of Pub. Safety*, 401 Mass. 418, 424 (1988) (proposed rules 801(d)(2)(D) and 403); *Simmons v. Yurchak*, 28 Mass. App. 371, 374 (1990) (proposed rule 803(3)).

9. The *Guide*, which is updated annually, is available on the Massachusetts courts website at http://www.mass.gov/courts/case-legal-res/guidelines/mass-guide-to-evidence/. A PDF version of the 2016 edition is available at http://www.mass.gov/courts/docs/sjc/guide-to-evidence/massguidetoevidence.pdf.

law of evidence."[10] Rather, the purpose of the *Guide* is "to make the law of evidence more understandable to the bench, bar, and public."[11] The *Guide* is not law, however, so in the words of one blogger, "the *Guide to Evidence* should be the first (but not the last) place any lawyer with an evidentiary question should go to get a handle on the law."[12] Thus, when you research the law of evidence, begin with the *Guide*, but continue to use treatises—and your skills in researching cases.

III. Massachusetts Court Rules

A. Courts That Promulgate Rules

Although the SJC is the only court that establishes rules applicable in all the courts of the Commonwealth, the lower courts have authority to promulgate rules for proceedings before them. In addition to formal rules, many courts issue standing orders relating to proceedings. These are, in effect, rules. Table 10-1 shows Massachusetts courts that promulgate rules and issue standing orders.

Table 10-1. Massachusetts Courts That Promulgate Rules and Issue Standing Orders

Supreme Judicial Court	Housing Court
Appeals Court	Juvenile Court
Trial Court	Land Court
Superior Court	Probate and Family Court
District Court	Superior Court
Boston Municipal Court	

B. Sources for Massachusetts Rules

1. Print Sources

Rules adopted by the SJC are included in the print volumes of the official *Massachusetts Reports*. This is the official source for the Massachusetts Rules

---

10. Statement of the Supreme Judicial Court, *Massachusetts Guide to Evidence* at ii (Supreme Judicial Court 2008). The Statement of the SJC on the *Guide* is available at http://www.mass.gov/courts/case-legal-res/guidelines/mass-guide-to-evidence/statement-from-the-supreme-judicial-court-and-introduction.html.

11. *Id.*

12. This blog can be found at http://masslawblog.com/courts/the-very-confusing-state-of-the-law-of-evidence-in-massachusetts/. The authors of the treatise on evidence in the *Massachusetts Practice Series* publish a guide to the *Guide*: Hon. William G. Young, John R. Pollets & Christopher Poreda, *Annotated Guide to Massachusetts Evidence, 2016 Edition* (*Massachusetts Practice Series*, Vol. 20A, West 2016).

of Civil Procedure, the Massachusetts Rules of Criminal Procedure, the Massachusetts Rules of Appellate Procedure, and the Rules of the Massachusetts Supreme Judicial Court. Because it is very difficult to find and update rules using these print volumes, lawyers almost universally use unofficial sources for court rules.

Compilations of Massachusetts court rules are available in print from several publishers. Among them are the following:

- *Massachusetts Lawyers Weekly*, a newspaper, publishes rules when they are promulgated. Its parent company, Lawyers Weekly Publications, publishes an annual volume entitled *The Rules*, which includes the rules of civil, criminal, and appellate procedure, and the rules and standing orders of all the courts listed in Table 10-1. In addition, it includes rules from other state quasi-judicial bodies and rules of local federal courts but does not include case annotations. To complement this volume, Lawyers Weekly offers subscribers to its rules service online access to rules and e-mail alerts of new rules or amendments.

- LexisNexis publishes annually a two-volume, annotated rules edition. It includes the rules of civil, criminal, and appellate procedure, and the rules of all the courts listed in Table 10-1. This set includes case annotations and research references, and has an index.

- West publishes annually a two-volume set that has a federal volume and a state volume. The federal volume includes the Federal Rules of Civil Procedure, the Federal Rules of Appellate Procedure, and the Federal Rules of Evidence, in addition to rules of local federal courts. The state volume has the Massachusetts rules of civil, criminal, and appellate procedure, and the rules and standing orders of the courts listed in Table 10-1 as well as rules of some quasi-judicial bodies. This set is updated by the *Massachusetts Interim Annotation Service* pamphlets and by the *Massachusetts Legislative Service*.

2. Electronic Sources

The website of the Massachusetts court system provides links to the rules of the courts. The website states, "If there are discrepancies between the electronic versions of the rules found on this website and the official print versions that appear in a volume such as *Massachusetts Reports*, the print version should be considered authoritative." The website provides links to e-books of rules of many Massachusetts courts to make them accessible on electronic devices without the need for internet access.[13]

Commercial services also provide access to Massachusetts court rules and standing orders. Lexis Advance has a source, "MA-Massachusetts State and Federal Court Rules," that includes rules of Massachusetts courts and local rules of federal courts sitting in Massachusetts, with annotations and references. This source is updated as the materials are received. As with other Lexis Advance sources, this source has an expandable, searchable table of contents, which you can use to gain direct access to the material you are searching for. To locate Massachusetts court rules on Westlaw, use the Browse feature to get access to the table of contents of the Massachusetts Statutes and Court Rules database. Check as of when the database is current by clicking on the "i" icon for the database. On Bloomberg Law, browse to "State Laws and Regulations" and then to Massachusetts court rules.

3. Sources for Massachusetts Rules of Professional Conduct

The Massachusetts Rules of Professional Conduct are set forth in Rule 3:07 of the SJC Rules. Thus, you can locate these rules using the sources discussed above. An additional source for these rules is the website of the Board of Bar Overseers and the Office of the Bar Counsel.[14] The Board of Bar Overseers and the Office of the Bar Counsel are independent administrative bodies established by the SJC to investigate and evaluate complaints against lawyers. The website includes links to the rules of professional conduct and to other rules relating to the practice of law in Massachusetts. It is also a source of other important material relating to legal ethics and lawyer discipline in Massachusetts.

C. Using Court Rules

In working with rules, use the skills you use to work with statutes. First, read the rule carefully. If it is complex, outline it or create a flow chart.

Then, update the rule to make sure you have the rule as it is currently in effect. One way to update a rule is to get in touch with the clerk of court. To confirm that you have the current version of the rule, the clerk may be willing to send you the rule by e-mail or fax. If not, visit the clerk's office at the courthouse to obtain a copy of the rule. If you use a commercial service, be sure to assess the extent to which the rules database is updated.

---

13. See http://www.mass.gov/courts/case-legal-res/law-lib/laws-by-source/ebooks/.
14. The address is http://www.mass.gov/obcbbo/rules.htm.

When you apply a court rule, you may need to go beyond the text of the rule to locate and analyze cases or other material interpreting it. How extensively you research a court rule depends on the purpose for which you are doing the research.

If you are researching court rules to find specific requirements for citing Massachusetts authority in a brief to a Massachusetts appellate court, you probably need to go no further than to read carefully Rule 16(g) of the Massachusetts Rules of Appellate Procedure. If, on the other hand, you represent an attorney who is subject to a bar disciplinary proceeding after having failed repeatedly to comply with court orders to pay child support, you need to look further than the text of the rule. You would likely read cases interpreting Rule 8.4(c) and (e) of the Rules of Professional Conduct to see what conduct has been found to involve "dishonesty, fraud, deceit, or misrepresentation" or be "prejudicial to the administration of justice," and you would also read cases under Rule 8.4(h) to determine what type of conduct has been held "to adversely reflect on … fitness to practice law."

In addition, you may find material analogous to legislative history, for example, notes or comments by the commission or other body that drafted the rule or amendment. For example, the operative provisions of the Rules of Professional Conduct are preceded by a preamble explaining generally the reasons underlying the rules and by a note concerning their scope. Each rule is followed by an official comment. This material may help you interpret the rules.

Material accompanying changes to a rule may also be helpful. For example, revisions to Rule 31(b) of the Massachusetts Rules of Criminal Procedure and to Rule 6(b)(2) of the Massachusetts Rules of Appellate Procedure were preceded by a report of the Standing Committee on the Rules of Criminal Procedure recommending changes and stating reasons for the proposed changes. This material may contribute to your understanding of the meaning of the rule.

IV. Federal Court Rules

An extensive body of rules exists at the federal level. These rules are published in many of the sources discussed above as well as in publications of federal statutes. Courts frequently post their rules on their websites. For example, the U.S. Supreme Court's rules are on its website.[15] Among other sources of federal

---

15. The website is http://www.supremecourt.gov/ctrules/ctrules.aspx.

rules are Lexis Advance, Westlaw, and Bloomberg Law. A federal court may have its own "local rules" with specific practices required by that court. Even though these rules are rules of federal courts, local rules are frequently available in compilations of state court rules.

Appendix A

Basics of Citation

I. Why Citation Is So Important

Citation in legal writing is essential because of the importance of authority in legal problem solving. Citation tells the reader *which* authority supports the writer's analysis or argument and *how* the authority supports it. Because this information is so important to the legal reader, citations to authority ordinarily appear within the text of law-practice documents instead of in footnotes.[1]

This appendix gives a very general introduction to legal citation and identifies Massachusetts specifics. For detailed treatment, refer to one of the two main citation manuals, *The Bluebook* and the *ALWD Guide*.[2] As an alternative, refer to a text on legal citation.[3]

---

1. Bryan Garner, a leading author on legal writing style, argues that citations in legal writing should be moved to footnotes to "unclutter" documents. Bryan A. Garner, *Legal Writing in Plain English* § 23 (U. of Chi. Press 2001). In general, however, legal readers and writers do not see citation as clutter, but rather as essential information about the force of the proposition for which the authority is cited. Thus, in legal documents citation has a purpose different from, or additional to, the purpose of citation in, for example, an historical essay. Given this importance, as a general rule lawyers and judges continue to cite to authority within the text of documents.

2. The two most widely adopted citation manuals are *The Bluebook: A Uniform System of Citation* (The Columbia Law Review et al. eds., 20th ed., 2015) (*The Bluebook*) and Association of Legal Writing Directors & Coleen M. Barger, *ALWD Guide to Legal Citation* (5th ed., Wolters Kluwer Law & Business 2014) (*ALWD Guide*).

3. For a guide to *The Bluebook*, see Linda J. Barris, *Understanding and Mastering the Bluebook* (3d ed. 2015). For separate workbooks on the *ALWD Guide* and *The Bluebook*, see books by Tracy McGaugh Norton et al.: *Interactive Citation Workbook for ALWD Guide to Legal Citation, 2015 Edition* (2015) or *Interactive Citation Workbook for The Bluebook: A Uniform System of Citation, 2015 Edition* (2015).

II. Sources of Citation Rules

Legal writers follow standard rules of citation to enable readers to locate cited material easily. Some of these rules are set by courts.[4] Other rules are "codified" in the citation systems prescribed in the two main citation manuals.

In some jurisdictions, court rules require use of one of the two citation manuals for papers filed in court. Massachusetts does not impose this requirement, and the current editions of *The Bluebook* and the *ALWD Guide* produce identical citations. Some employers have internal conventions for citing authority. If no system is specified, choose one, learn its rules, and use it consistently.

Court rules and citation manuals are very specific about detail, so refer to them whenever you cite—until you are confident that you have memorized the rules. For papers filed in court, local court rules override rules in citation manuals.

The Office of the Reporter of Decisions has prepared a Massachusetts *Style Manual*, which is available in PDF format on the reporter's website.[5] Citation is among the matters the *Style Manual* addresses. Although the *Style Manual* is used by the justices of the Supreme Judicial Court, their law clerks, and the staff of the Office of the Reporter of Decisions, there is no requirement that others follow it.

III. How a Citation Identifies Authority

A citation identifies an authority by giving its name and telling the reader where to find it. This information makes it possible for a reader to follow up on the citation—to locate and read the cited authority in print or online. Most standard citation formats point to the print version of an authority if there is one. As a general rule, if an authority is available both in print and online, you can retrieve the authority online by searching for the print citation.

The various types of authority are published differently, so identifying information in a citation varies by type of authority. Citation rules prescribe precisely what information must be included in a citation to a case, to a statute, to a regulation, and to other types of primary authority. They also prescribe

---

4. For example, a citation in a brief filed in a Massachusetts appellate court "shall include, wherever reasonably possible, a reference to any official report of the case." Mass. R. App. P. 16(g).

5. The website is http://www.mass.gov/courts/court-info/sjc/about/reporter-of-decisions/.

the specific format for each type of primary authority. Citation rules also prescribe the required information and format for citations to various types of secondary authority.[6]

To identify a case that has a print version, the citation provides at least the following information: 1) the name of the case; 2) at least one print reporter in which the reader can find the case, including the volume of the reporter; 3) the initial page of the case; 4) the page or pages where the reader can find specific support for the analysis or argument for which the case is cited; and 5) in parentheses, the year of decision. The date parenthetical includes an abbreviation for the court that decided the case if this information is not clear from the name of the reporter. Figure A-1 shows an example of a citation labeled to show its components.

Figure A-1. Components of a Case Citation

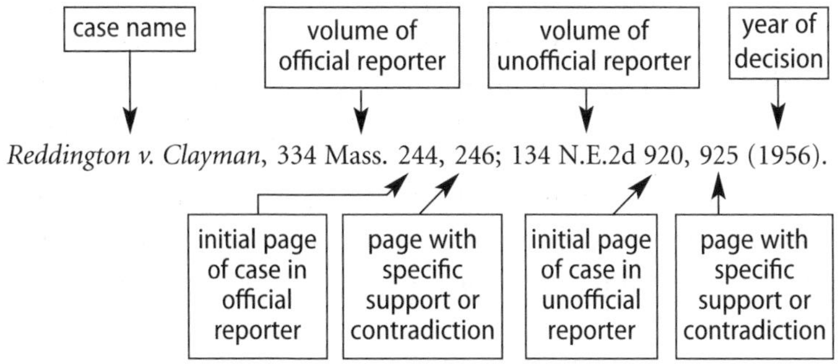

With the information in the citation to the *Reddington* case in Figure A-1, you could locate the case by pulling from a library shelf volume 334 of the *Massachusetts Reports* or volume 134 of the *North Eastern Reporter, Second Series* and opening to the first page of the case. You could also use Lexis Advance, Westlaw, or Bloomberg Law to retrieve the case by typing the citation into the appropriate search box. In addition, you could use the citation to search for the case in another commercial research service or on a free internet resource.

In Massachusetts, general laws are identified by chapter and section. Thus, you could locate the Massachusetts burglary statute with the information in

---

6. Note that both *The Bluebook* and the *ALWD Guide* have two citation formats: one is for law-practice documents and the other is for law review footnotes.

the following citation: Mass. Gen. Laws ch. 266, § 14. Citation rules generally require or prefer citation to the official code[7] and require that the citation include the code's date of publication. This information allows you to locate the statute in a print code by first skimming the spines of the set to locate the volume that includes this chapter and section, and then opening to section 14 of chapter 266. You could also use this information to retrieve the statute from Lexis Advance, Westlaw, Bloomberg Law, other commercial research services, or free internet resources.

IV. How a Citation Indicates the Way an Authority Supports a Proposition

A powerful feature of legal citation is the use of signals to indicate the relationship of the authority cited to the proposition that it supports or contradicts. An authority may support your analysis or argument directly or indirectly, specifically or generally, or in several other ways. Or, you may cite an authority to show that it contradicts or otherwise fails to support a proposition stated in a document. A citation signal conveys this information through a single word, phrase, or abbreviation. Because signals convey so much information so efficiently, effective use of the shorthand language of citation signals can contribute significantly to the precision and conciseness of your analysis or argument. Thus, it is worth investing the time and energy necessary to master citation signals.

In both main citation systems, the absence of a signal indicates that the cited authority directly supports the proposition for which it is cited. Both systems have signals that indicate varying degrees of indirect support (for example, *see*) and contradiction (for example, *but see*) and a signal to indicate general support (for example, *see generally*). When you use these signals, you should include a parenthetical explanation at the end of the citation to help the reader understand more precisely how the cited authority supports or contradicts the proposition for which you cite it.

The two main citation systems use the same signals to convey virtually the same information. Until you are confident that you have memorized the rules in the manual you are using, make a habit of referring to the manual.

---

7. In briefs filed in a Massachusetts appellate court, a statute must be cited to "the official publication containing statutory ... material." Mass. R. App. P. 16(g).

V. Massachusetts Specifics

The only citation form requirements that are binding under Massachusetts law are set forth in Rule 16(g) of the Massachusetts Rules of Appellate Procedure. That rule states a preference for including the citation to the official source for Massachusetts cases, statutes, and "similar material." The rule provides that, in briefs filed with an appellate court,

> Massachusetts Reports between 17 Massachusetts and 97 Massachusetts shall be cited by the name of the reporter. Any other citation shall include, wherever reasonably possible, a reference to any official report of the case or to the official publication containing statutory or similar material. References to decisions and other authorities should include, in addition to the page at which the decision or section begins, a page reference to the particular material therein upon which reliance is placed, and the year of the decision; as, for example: 334 Mass. 593, 597–598 (1956). Quotations of Massachusetts statutory material shall include a citation to either the Acts and Resolves of Massachusetts or to the current edition of the General Laws published pursuant to a resolve of the General Court.

Rule 16(g) of Massachusetts District/Municipal Courts Appellate Division Appeals Rules has identical language.

Basics of Full-Text Searching on Lexis Advance, Westlaw, and Bloomberg Law

The chapters in this book discuss commercial research services mainly in the context of Massachusetts sources. This appendix gives a general overview of full-text searching in the three most widely used commercial research services, Lexis Advance, Westlaw, and Bloomberg Law. For more in-depth treatment, consult materials prepared by these services or one of their representatives. Some information in this appendix may also be helpful when you use other commercial research services, such as Casemaker, Fastcase, Ravel Law, and VersusLaw.

Although this appendix addresses only full-text searching, Lexis Advance, Westlaw, and Bloomberg Law offer other research approaches. For examples, these services provide browsable tables of contents for many of their sources, and they allow you to search for case law by subject.

I. Steps in Full-Text Searching

To conduct an effective full-text search, you must take several general steps and many specific ones. Where you begin depends on where you are in your research process when you turn to one of these services. Table B-1 identifies six general steps for effective full-text searching.

Table B-1. Steps for Effective Full-Text Searching

Step #1	Choose a source for your search.
Step #2	Decide whether to use terms-and-connectors or natural-language searching.
Step #3	Construct a search.
Step #4	Evaluate your results.
Step #5	Modify your search, if necessary.
Step #6	Keep track of your searches.

A. Step #1: Choose a Source

The leading commercial research services divide their resources into collections of materials organized by jurisdiction, topic, and type of document. Although the services use different labels for these collections of materials, we refer to them as "sources." Your choice of a source determines the material that the research service will search. Thus, choosing a source is a crucial step: no matter how well you craft your search, if you search in the wrong place you will not find what you are looking for. To make an appropriate choice, you must have a good preliminary understanding of your problem. Chapter 2 discusses how to gain a preliminary understanding of a problem.

Your choice of a source may also affect the cost of your research. If you have a subscription to certain sources, then accessing documents beyond those sources may incur costs. In addition, accessing documents in sources outside your subscription can be especially costly in more comprehensive or specialized sources. Before planning research beyond your subscription, be sure to consider the potential costs. You may retrieve cost information through the information icon for a particular source, or through your service's pricing guide or an account representative.

1. Questions to Help You Choose a Source

As you begin to search for a source, ask yourself the following preliminary questions:

- Am I searching for primary or secondary sources?
- Is the issue controlled by federal or state law?
- If the issue is controlled by state law, which state's law controls?

- Am I doing a general search for authority or am I looking for a specific type of authority?
- If I am looking for a specific type of authority, which type am I looking for (e.g., cases, statutes)?

Once you answer these questions, look within the service for a source that includes the type of material you are looking for. For this search, Lexis Advance, Westlaw, and Bloomberg Law allow you to conduct a full-text search or browse a directory. All three services have both very broad and very narrow sources, and all three allow you to run a search in multiple sources (e.g., searching for statutes and regulations simultaneously).

2. Choosing a Source on Lexis Advance

Lexis Advance offers several ways for you to choose a source. First, you may browse the hierarchy of sources and sort that hierarchy by type of authority, jurisdiction, or practice area. Second, you may use the drop-down menu beside the search bar to narrow your search by jurisdiction, type of authority, or practice area. Finally, you may search for specific sources by typing a name or description in the search bar. This will generate a drop-down list of potential sources. Once you find an appropriate source, select the source to add it as a filter for your search.

Knowing what material is within a source is crucial. You can only be sure that you are searching in the right place if you know what substantive material the source contains and how frequently the source is updated. The answers to those questions may require you to search in different, or additional, sources. To check the coverage of a source, click that source's information icon to see the coverage of the source and other potentially helpful information.

3. Choosing a Source on Westlaw

You may choose a source on Westlaw in several ways. First, you may browse the hierarchy of sources and sort the hierarchy by type of authority, jurisdiction, or practice area. Second, you may use the drop-down menu beside the search bar to limit your search by jurisdiction. Finally, you may describe the source in the search bar to see a drop-down menu of potential sources. To check the coverage of a source in Westlaw, click on the source's information icon.

4. Choosing a Source on Bloomberg Law

Bloomberg Law offers several ways to choose a source. First, you may browse the directory of available sources and sort that directory by jurisdiction, content type, or practice area. Second, you may describe the source you wish to find in the search bar, and choose a source from the drop-down list that appears. To check the coverage of a source in Bloomberg Law, click on the information icon next to the name of the source in the directory.

B. Step #2: Terms and Connectors or Natural Language?

Both Lexis Advance and Westlaw allow you to search using terms and connectors or natural language. Bloomberg Law only allows terms-and-connectors searches. How do you decide which technique to use for a given search?

1. Terms-and-Connectors Searching

When you use search using terms and connectors, you construct a search that includes both search terms and "connectors," symbols or words that tell the research service where the search terms must occur in relation to each other in the documents retrieved. Terms-and-connectors searching is sometimes referred to as "Boolean" searching.

A terms-and-connectors search locates *all* the documents within the selected source that have your search terms in the precise relationship prescribed by your search. But a terms-and-connectors search will locate *only* these documents. Thus, using terms and connectors is an effective search technique only when you are familiar with the topic and with the language used in the type of document you are seeking.

Because you must be able to predict the document's language, and to some extent its syntax, terms-and-connectors searching is generally more effective when you are searching for expository documents, like cases and some secondary sources, than when you are searching for statutes or regulations. It is often difficult to predict the precise language in a statute or a regulation; thus, a search technique that demands less precision may be more effective when you are searching for these materials.

2. Natural-Language Searching

A natural-language search uses the ordinary language you would use to describe what you are looking for to another person. You are probably familiar with this type of search from using Google or other online search engines. When you type a natural-language search, the research service processes your search using its proprietary algorithm.

Natural-language searching is useful at the beginning of a research project, or at any time when you are unfamiliar with a topic or the language used in documents you are looking for. Because a natural-language search is not comprehensive, it is not appropriate when you need to be sure you have located every relevant document.

C. Step #3: Construct a Search

1. Constructing a Terms-and-Connectors Search

Develop the habit of constructing searches offline, with pencil and paper or in a word processing document. This habit will prevent you from running a search before you are ready and wasting time and money on irrelevant search results.

a. Generate Search Terms

To begin, generate a comprehensive list of search terms by following the suggestions in Chapter 2. Because a terms-and-connectors search will locate only documents that include the precise terms you include in your search, try to include more rather than fewer terms on your list, at least for an initial search. Include both general and specific terms as well as synonyms. For example, to search for cases on the enforceability of an agreement in advance of marriage to protect assets of one spouse in the event of divorce, you would include "prenuptial," "antenuptial," "contract," and "agreement." You would also probably include the terms "enforce," "uphold," "valid," "spouse," "husband," and "wife."

Next, modify the search terms with expanders and placeholders to locate variations of your words. The exclamation point expands words beyond a common root. For example, *enforc!* will find enforce, enforceable, enforceability, enforced, enforcing, etc.

The asterisk or question mark serves as a placeholder for an individual letter. Up to three asterisks can be used in a single term. This symbol is helpful when you are not sure which form of the word is used, or when you are not sure of the spelling of a word. For example, the search term *dr*nk* will find drink, drank, and drunk. (On Lexis Advance, use the symbol ? instead of * to hold a place in the middle of a word.) Placeholders are preferable to the expander in some instances. Using an expander on *trad!* with hopes of finding *trade*, *trading*, *trades*, etc. will also produce results that include *traditional*. A better search term may be *trad****.

To retrieve all variations of compound terms, use a hyphen to connect the parts. For example, use *on-line* rather than *online*.

b. Add Connectors

Using connectors effectively is essential to efficient terms-and-connectors searching. Connectors prescribe where search terms are located in relation to one another in targeted documents. Even minimally sophisticated combinations of the various connectors and parentheses, which indicate to the service the order in which connectors should be processed, can increase the effectiveness of your searches. Table B-2 shows the most basic connectors used by Lexis Advance, Westlaw, and Bloomberg Law.

Table B-2. Basic Connectors for Terms-and-Connectors Searching

Connector	What It Retrieves
and	documents containing two or more terms anywhere in the document
or	documents containing either of two terms anywhere in the document
/n	documents containing two terms within n words in the document
/p	documents containing two terms within the same paragraph (Lexis Advance interprets this as /75)
/s	documents containing two terms within the same sentence (Lexis Advance interprets this as /25)

For additional and more sophisticated connectors, consult materials available from Lexis Advance, Westlaw, and Bloomberg Law.

Although most connectors are the same for the three services, two differences can cause some confusion. The first difference involves the connector "or." Westlaw interprets a blank space as the connector "or." However, Lexis Advance usually treats two words connected by a blank space as if they were inside quotation marks. And Bloomberg Law treats a blank space as the connector "and." To avoid potential confusion across services, get into the habit of typing "or," which works on all three services. The second difference involves searching for a specific phrase. Lexis Advance interprets a blank space as joining words in a phrase. By contrast, to search for a phrase on Westlaw or Bloomberg Law, you must enclose the phrase in quotation marks. Again, to avoid confusion, use quotation marks to search for phrases on all three services.

c. Type Your Search in the Search Box

After adding connectors, you are ready to run your search. Lexis Advance and Westlaw automatically treat searches that contain connectors as terms-and-connectors searches rather than natural-language searches. Bloomberg Law only recognizes terms-and-connectors searches at this time.

d. Restrict Your Search

All three services allow you to restrict your terms-and-connectors search to specific parts of documents, such as the date, author, or court. Lexis Advance calls these subparts *segments*; Westlaw and Bloomberg Law call them *fields*. Choose the advanced search option on Lexis Advance and Westlaw to see a template allowing you to search segments or fields. Bloomberg Law's template of available fields appears below the search bar.[1]

e. Run Your Search

To avoid potentially costly errors, be sure to proofread your search before you run it. Now you are ready to click on the search button to run your search.

2. Constructing a Natural-Language Search

Natural-language searching is more intuitive than terms-and-connectors searching. As with a terms-and-connectors search, you must generate search terms. For this task, natural-language searching requires less precision than terms-and-connectors searching. This is why natural-language searching is generally preferable when you are unfamiliar with a topic. But since your search is less precise, a natural-language search is likely to yield results that are less focused than the results of a terms-and-connectors search. Once you gain greater familiarity with your problem, you can restrict your search to yield more precise results. Both Lexis Advance and Westlaw treat your searches as natural-language searches unless they contain connectors. Bloomberg Law does not allow natural-language searching at this time.

D. Step #4: Evaluate Your Results

1. Understanding the Display

All three services allow you to choose how to sort the results of your search. The default display order is by relevance to your search, although Lexis Advance

---

1. Currently, Bloomberg Law's template appears only if you begin by clicking the "Search and Browse" tab and then selecting one of the "Specialized Searches." If you select "All Legal Content," the fields template will not appear.

and Westlaw let you change that default. Each service uses its own proprietary algorithm to determine which documents are most relevant to your search. You may choose other sorting options that vary by service. Lexis Advance allows you to sort by date, level of court, jurisdiction, or document title. Westlaw allows you to sort by date, most cited documents (based on citations in other legal authorities), and most used documents (based on aggregate usage by Westlaw customers). Bloomberg Law allows you to sort by date, court, and most cited documents.

2. Working with Documents

All three services allow you to assess the relevance of a document without necessarily reading it from beginning to end. For example, if you search for cases, the result list will display the case name as well as short excerpts from the case that contain your search terms, although there may be may other relevant excerpts in the case. Second, once you open a document in your search results, each service allows you to navigate through each occurrence of the term within the document.

3. Saving, Printing, Downloading, or E-mailing Results

Lexis Advance, Westlaw, and Bloomberg Law offer ways to annotate documents and save them in online folders. Some researchers may find these services compatible with their work habits, while others may prefer to save and annotate documents on their own computers or in print. Consult each service for details.

In addition, all three services allow you to download or e-mail documents instead of printing them. When working with a document offline, you can locate your search terms within the document by using the "Find" function in your word processing application. Moreover, now that most word processing applications allow highlighting and in-line annotating, you may choose to read and organize your research documents entirely on your computer.

Once you identify a document as relevant, consider printing it. You must read (and often re-read) relevant documents very carefully. Many researchers find studying a document on paper more comfortable and effective than studying it on a computer screen.

E. Step #5: Modify Your Search

1. Narrowing a Result List Using Filters and Additional Search Terms

If your initial search yields results that are promising but too numerous or too general, all three services allow you to choose from various filters to narrow your list of results. For example, you may limit your results by jurisdiction, court, date, or topic. In addition, on Lexis Advance and Westlaw the "Search Within Results" feature allows you to construct a search within a search to narrow your initial search results. Users may research efficiently by constructing a broad initial search and then taking several different approaches to filtering the search. The "Search Within Results" feature does not support natural-language searching.

2. Editing Your Search

If a search produces no results, edit your search by using broader connectors (for example, search for terms in the same paragraph rather than in the same sentence) or alternative terms. Consider also running your search in a more comprehensive source or in multiple sources.

If a search produces results that seem irrelevant, skim some of the results to try to figure out why. Skimming results will help you decide how to edit your search—by using wholly different search terms or by omitting broad terms or using more restrictive connectors. Consider also using a different or narrower set of sources.

F. Step #6: Keep Track of Your Searches

Even after you become experienced in online searching, you should still keep track of your searches. Keeping records of the dates you searched, the searches you ran, and your search results will help you stay on track and avoid duplicating your research. Your notes will also indicate how far back in time you need to go to update your research as you near your project deadline.

All three services allow you to store records of past searches and results for a period of time. Check the service you are using to determine for how long these records are stored. To view these records on Lexis Advance and Westlaw, click "History." On Bloomberg Law, click "Research Trail." All three services allow you to print these records. Getting into a habit of printing them is a very simple way to keep track of your research.

II. Steps After Your Full-Text Search

Using a full-text search to compile a list of relevant authorities is but one research task among many. Re-read Chapter 2 to review where full-text searching fits within the overall process of legal research.

Appendix C

Selected Bibliography — Books on General Legal Research

J.D.S. Armstrong & Christopher A. Knott, *Where the Law Is: An Introduction to Advanced Legal Research* (4th ed. 2012).

Steven M. Barkan, Barbara Bintliff & Mary Whisner, *Fundamentals of Legal Research* (10th ed. 2015).

Robert C. Berring & Elizabeth Edinger, *Finding the Law* (12th ed. 2005).

Morris Cohen & Kent Olson, *Legal Research in a Nutshell* (11th ed. 2013).

Christina L. Kunz, Deborah A. Schmedemann, Anne L. Bateson, Matthew P. Downs & Mehmet Konar-Steenberg, *The Process of Legal Research* (8th ed. 2012).

Laurel Currie Oates & Anne Enquist, *Just Research* (4th ed. 2012).

Amy E. Sloan, *Basic Legal Research* (6th ed. 2015).

About the Authors

E. Joan Blum has taught Legal Reasoning, Research, and Writing at Boston College Law School since 1985. She has taught in Bosnia and Herzegovina on behalf of the U.S. Department of Justice and in the International Tax Program at Harvard. She is Faculty Director of the Boston College Law Summer Institute: Foundations of U.S. Law and Practice.

Shaun B. Spencer has directed the Legal Skills Program at the University of Massachusetts School of Law since 2011. He previously taught legal research and writing at Harvard Law School and advanced legal writing at Boston College Law School. His scholarly interests include the empirical study of legal writing and information privacy law.

Index